SURVIVING
LOSS

HOW TO NAVIGATE PAIN, ATTRACT
DIVINE FAVOUR, FIND PEACE AND
THRIVE IN A PURPOSE-FILLED LIFE

EUNICE KEMUNTO

Copyright © 2020 Eunice Kemunto
All rights reserved.

Scripture quotations, unless otherwise indicated, are taken from the Holy Bible, New International Version ®, NIV ®. Copyright © 1973, 1978, 1984, 2011 by Biblica, Inc.™ Used by permission of Zondervan. All rights reserved worldwide. www.zondervan.com. The "NIV" and "New International Version" are trademarks registered in the United States Patent and Trademark Office by Biblica, Inc.™

Scripture quotations marked (KJV) are from the Authorized (King James) Version. Rights in the Authorized Version in the United Kingdom are vested in the Crown. Reproduced by permission of the Crown's patentee, Cambridge University Press.

ISBN: 978-1-7770932-0-4

WHAT OTHERS ARE SAYING ABOUT *SURVIVING LOSS:*

"Greetings!
Your book, entitled 'Surviving Loss,' will awaken talents, gifts, visions and skills in women/men who have/or are suffering from abuse, separation, pains, threats, sorrows, bitterness or other conditions indecent to a civilized culture. This book will enlighten people who are in the wilderness that it is not the end of life; the wilderness is a place of preparation that God will use to marshal you into the prepared place of honor and dignity. Please accept my appreciation for your preferment to review your book."

Samuel J. Brown
Pastor in Liberia

"'Surviving Loss' is a page turner, especially if you have a heavy heart or questions about your purpose in life and what the Lord has in mind for you. Eunice frankly tells about the challenges and opposition she has faced and how the power of prayer and living righteously increased her favour in Jesus Christ and how she was miraculously blessed beyond her expectations.

She teaches that 'for every pain, there's a purpose,' and I say amen to those words of wisdom. Too often we think the Lord has forsaken us when we are afflicted with loss or change, but as Eunice teaches, we are pruned. Whom the Lord loves, He chastens. We can then become a modern Mary, Elizabeth, Esther or Ruth, a woman who praises Christ and trusts in His timing and organization."

Susan Harper
Elementary school music teacher

"Loss is something that can either make or break you. I believe that it is among those parts of human lives that we are never prepared for. Yet there are those who come out of loss refined like diamond. Again, there are those who get shattered into pieces that can never be placed back together forever. This entirely depends on the approach one decides to give the loss they are experiencing.

Eunice takes us through her personal life, which I must admit is courageous. She is a woman who has faced loss of her marriage, jobs, happiness and peace. She seeks help from therapists as she battles with suicidal thoughts. She tries to forget her problems with the use of alcohol, but up until she raises her hands in surrender to the Supreme Power of God, she was unable to get help.

Her story is woven of loss and eventual restoration from God, which I will call victories. She gives her testimonies of a restored marriage and finding a suitable job in addition to other people's testimonies who also experienced God even in their loss.

Through the book she examines real-life examples that one can relate with. There is a woman whose son faces a death or life situation when he was trying to follow up on his stolen money. The different chapters handle steps in which someone can handle loss in an elaborate manner. Apart from that, it draws biblical examples, which confirm that loss is inevitable to every human being.

This is a book that does not allow us to wallow in pity party and despair but helps us understand how to draw nearer to God despite our brokenness. It confirms a simple message that yes, we will face pain out of loss but giving up is not an option.

I would recommend this book to every one of us who is facing loss of any kind. It is comforting because it reminds you about The Supreme Creator. It makes you understand that it is not yet over until God says so. Most importantly, the book taught me that prayer should be our job description in this world in order to stay aware of Satan's perils."

Rumona Opiyo
Literature Enthusiast/Book Reviewer/Writer

"Dear Sister Eunice Kemunto,

May God bless you abundantly for this beautiful manuscript. I have gone through this book, 'Surviving Loss,' and all through my reading, I have been shedding tears. I am a lady who has been struggling with brokenness in my relationships; I am 33 and still single, all dating ending to disappointments, the latest one being May this year after being in it for two years. I am a staunch Adventist, and in regular standing. I am a P1 teacher and newly employed by the government this year. I thank God for this job.

Your inspiration is real, the themes are very powerful and the incredible testimonies in here have uplifted me. I am certain you are God-sent to me because I have been desperate and questioning God what is wrong with all these disappointments, but now I feel rejuvenated again and I want to trust God and wait upon His blessings. I assure you, dear, this book is beyond blessings. It is unique, rich and expounding on themes that are encouraging us despite of our spiritual low due to different circumstances in our daily lives.

I will be glad to connect with you for more coaching and for spiritual encouragement.
Thanks, and be blessed.

Yours,
Egla Kemunto Nyabwana"

"This second installment of her book 'Surviving Loss,' which follows her first book 'Broken but Blessed,' is very engaging and you cannot help but marvel at how her story continues on while providing encouragement and support to anyone that takes the time to read and absorb such insightful words. This book is full of encouragement and spurs you on to see yourself through the eyes of the Lord and His utmost perfect will for our lives. A very good read whether you are reading to the end or reading a bit at a time. When you are surviving loss, especially when your losses have multiplied, these words of encouragement will soothe your soul and remind you of how much you are loved and valued by the one who carries us through when we cannot take another step."

Noella Baird,
RN, BSN

"I love Eunice's honesty in sharing her story in 'Surviving Loss.' She has been through significant loss, so her book is very personal and practical, not just theoretical. She is clearly passionate about helping others in similar situations. The way she weaves her journey and examples from the Bible will help readers navigate their own burdens and pain with God."

Megan Ryan
Editor

DEDICATION

My constant inspiration is my daughter, Princess Jessica. When I behold her beautiful face, my prayer is that she will grow to be a God-fearing woman of purpose and that the Lord's favourable hand will be outpoured upon her life in every season. And that this book, and its results, will make her proud to be its inspiration.

CONTENTS

Introduction 1

Part I: How To Navigate Pain 5

Chapter One: When Things Fall Apart 5
Chapter Two: Is This Fair? 20
Chapter Three: Whom He Loves He Prunes 33
Part I Workbook And Self-Assessment Questions 42

Part II: How To Attract Divine Favour 45

Chapter Four: Keys To Attract Divine Favour 45
Chapter Five: Favour And Faith 61
Chapter Six: Agents Of Favour 73
Part II Workbook And Self-Assessment Questions 84

Part III: How To Find Peace In The Storm 86

Chapter Seven: You Are Chosen 86
Chapter Eight: Be Consistent 98
Part III Workbook And Self-Assessment Questions 108

Part IV: Thriving In A Purpose-Filled Life 110

Chapter Nine: Hide And Seek 110
Chapter Ten: Beyond Blessed 121
Chapter Eleven: The Transformation 128
Part IV Workbook And Self-Assessment Questions 139

Works Cited 140
About The Author 141

INTRODUCTION

I wrote this book in the summer of 2019. I had been carrying around this book idea with me for several months. I guess the heat of summer coaxed it out of me. I am grateful that I was able to get it out and help thousands of women (and men) who are experiencing pain, depression, discouragement, disappointment, or despair as a result of divorce, losing a loved one through death, miscarriage, career breakdowns, marital challenges, financial breakdowns, health challenges, relationship breakdowns, and more.

After reading this book, my goal is that you will be able to receive healing from your pain and thrive in perfect peace amidst life's storms because all things are working together for your good.

Perhaps you have experienced or are experiencing a series of losses and have questions about when the time will come for you to finally get a break and enjoy a life of freedom, fullness, and fruitfulness. Perhaps your losses have caused you deep pain, anguish, and discouragement.

Eight years ago, I experienced depression, despair, and discouragement as a result of divorce. Nothing I tried in my own human effort could heal my wounds or relieve my pain. But I finally found my way into a new life of bliss and favour. In this book, I want to share with you my journey of how I survived my losses, hoping that I will help many women (men are welcome to read, too) to also survive their losses and attract divine favour.

None of us is immune to pain. Although pain comes naturally, dealing with it does not. Many of us find ourselves self-medicating it using addictive substances or behaviour, or masking it and pretending that everything is alright. Unfortunately, these strategies are only temporary and do not offer a lasting solution for us to live a life that is free, fruitful, and full. In this book, I weave my story with transparency using relatable examples from faith and culture and provide readers with the necessary tools to author their own process of dealing with pain and discovering their true inner strength.

If you are experiencing pain or loss or are wounded from the suffering you have gone through, this book is for you. The words herein will bring hope, healing, and transformation to your life, and the lives of your loved ones as you share this book.

Loss and pain confront all of us. The difference between a winner and a whiner is in the choices that we make when faced by pain. We can choose to whine and self-medicate by masking the pain, developing dysfunctional relationships and harmful addictions. Or be a winner by embracing the pain and navigating through it successfully by developing a winning mentality and thought process.

In Part One, we will look at how to navigate pain. I discuss the temporary solutions we often turn to when things fall apart and how to get at the core issues that really need healing. I will also address whether our suffering is fair and how God uses that suffering to encourage our growth.

In Part Two, I will teach you how to attract divine favour, which is God's powerful presence in your life. Favour is what opens doors that no man can shut. I discuss keys such as humility, vision, thanks-living, and right standing with God that will help you begin to attract divine favour consistently. You will also learn that favour requires faith and that God uses people and even losses to bring about miracles in your life.

Part Three focuses on finding perfect peace amidst storms of life. I want to reassure you that you are chosen by God. I also want to encourage you to be consistent even when you don't find positive results right away.
Part Four is about thriving in a purpose-filled life. I have discussed what happens when we resist the call of God.

Sometimes we resist His plan for our life and His process, which I have learned only wastes time. I also discuss how we are beyond blessed when we submit to God's will and how you can turn your deepest pain into something for God's glory.

Ready? Let us get into it...

*You can receive healing from your pain, and you can thrive in perfect peace amidst life's storms because **all** things are working together for your good.*

Have a question for the author? Send me your ideas, comments, and complaints.

I want to know what you think. You can reach me at: coach4survivingloss@gmail.com

PART I:

HOW TO NAVIGATE PAIN

Chapter One:

WHEN THINGS FALL APART

When things fall apart, it really is not the end; favour and blessings await you if you would only see things the way God sees them.

I had just experienced the Lord's miraculous and healing hand over my marriage. After six years of brokenness, I was restored, and my marriage healed. See *Broken but Blessed*, my first book. We were in a season of celebrating this victory over spiritual warfare and emotional exhaustion. As my husband and I soaked in the favour of God over our marriage, we told and retold stories about the events and circumstances of our lives for the past six years, lessons we had gleaned and so forth. I was unaware of the upcoming job loss.

The sad news hit me one morning when I had gone to work as usual only to be called to the employer's office. The purpose of the meeting was for her to suggest that she did not value my work and therefore was going to reduce my salary by a significant amount compared to what we had initially agreed to upon employment. As if that was not enough, I was humiliated when she mentioned that, in her opinion, I was not a well-seasoned accountant and therefore she needed to retrain me. This came as a surprise because all the while I worked for her, no concerns or warnings had been expressed. When you have been a hardworking and dedicated certified accountant for twelve years, doing the same things repeatedly, and someone mentions unsatisfactory work, it can be alarming. Our discussion did not go well at the end of the day, as I was not agreeable to the pay cut.

I left the office knowing that was the end of my job. I questioned why this job would go sour in these circumstances. Had I not prayed to God every morning asking that He would help me work with excellence like Joseph and give me good success like He did King Uzziah during his time?

When you are faced with inevitable loss or unexpected pain, emotions, thoughts, and questions suddenly overwhelm you. Why me? Why me again, Lord? Why now? Did I not pray for this job? Did I not give my best to this marriage? Was this not Your will for me? Did I not pray over my family's health and protection? You are left confused and unsure how to proceed, frightened, weary, and wasted. You are tempted to question what happened to God's blessings that make one rich without adding sorrow.

I did not reveal my job loss situation to my husband immediately as I did not want to suddenly end his celebrating mood. Eventually, I had to anyway as it was beginning to look obvious to him that I was not leaving the house for long hours on end. Thankfully, he did not condemn me after hearing the story. He sympathized and was supportive of me. "What next, Lord?" was my question. I had no desire to push out resumes applying for a new job. As days went by, I felt strongly the need to invest more of my time in ministry rather than pursuing full-time work. I know that when the Lord is pulling you from something or pushing you into something else, He will engineer the circumstances of your life to align with His will and purpose for your life. I prayed that God would clarify this for me.

The idea of writing my debut book, *Broken but Blessed*, was birthed at this time. Every day, I hit the library and just wrote away, as I now had enough time on my hands to dedicate to writing the manuscript of the book. Occasionally, I wondered where the funds to publish the book would come from as I had no income. The truth is that whom the Lord calls, He equips, and whom He equips, He sends. So, I obeyed His calling and trusted Him to provide in His own time. About two months later, my manuscript was completed. I prayed, asking for God's direction on what I should do next. When we ask God to direct our ways and lead our paths, He is faithful to do so. I know Him to be a God who would move heaven and earth to show us His will and plan for our lives. He does so step by step when we are obedient to Him.

One Sabbath, I went to church to worship, as was my custom. As I approached the church entrance, my spirit was strongly impressed to pick up the church bulletin that would normally have announcements. Usually, I did not pick up the bulletin, but this time was different. I soon discovered the reason for this—there was a job advert nicely tucked in the bottom of the announcements looking for a business manager for a school. Apparently, that advert had been there two Sabbaths prior and this was the final day the advert was being placed in the bulletin. Excited and elated, I strongly felt that this job was mine. Later, I quickly phoned the school to ask if they were still taking applications—the answer was yes. I prepared my job application and fired it off by email to the Adventist school.

Even though I felt strongly that this was the job God had in store for me, I occasionally worried as I did not hear back from the school for about three weeks. One of the nights that I was waiting, I dreamt about working at the conference of the Seventh-day Adventist schools, helping students with camp registrations. In the dream, I asked my boss if they had considered my resume, and he asked me to just send it in and they would consider it.

Now, I believe in dreams because I had previously dreamt about things that came to pass, though not in the exact way that I dreamt them. Before my marriage was restored, I had dreamt about it three times. The last time, I saw myself in a wedding gown and there was no groom in the wedding. Only my son, Joshua, and I were participating in the wedding, according to the dream. The maid of honor wanted us to hurry and leave before we were late; then I asked her in the dream where the groom was. Then an audible voice asked me, "Have you forgiven Richard?" (Richard is my husband's name.) At this, I knew the Lord was saying that Richard was my destined husband.

I waited for my new job to become a reality. On June 13, a co-applicant for the job who I knew personally mentioned to me that the school had requested her to submit her references for their regular background check. Usually whoever qualifies for the last step before hire gets to submit their references. I was utterly discouraged as I thought this lady was the one getting the job. In fact, that night I had no appetite for dinner. I asked

God what the meaning of this was. Had He not indicated to me in the dream that the job was mine?

When I woke up in the morning, I started my daily routine, and worship was in the centre of it. I listened to a sermon by one preacher I have respect for, Dr. Charles Stanley, and he was speaking from Isaiah 41:10 (KJV): "Fear thou not; for I am with thee: be not dismayed; for I am thy God: I will strengthen thee; yea, I will help thee; yea, I will uphold thee with the right hand of my righteousness." I believed this message with all my heart. All my fear, worry, anxiety, and discouragement disappeared. I believed that the Lord was working out something great for me.

One hour later on June 14, the phone rang. The caller identified herself and mentioned that she was sent by the school board to offer me the job at the Adventist school. Hurray! I was very happy. I sang praises to the Lord and prayed a thanksgiving prayer glorifying the almighty God for His mighty works and miraculous doings. His hand of favour was outpoured upon my life, despite the waiting process I had gone through. Friends, there are unexpected blessings that you can receive even in moments when you face defeat, discouragement and loss.

Our God is faithful to His faithful ones and to those who wait on Him. He will never leave nor forsake them in time of their need. June 19 was my start date for the new job. Now I had an income that would help finish the work He had started in me: the book. See Isaiah 40:31: "But those who hope in the LORD / will renew their strength. / They will soar on wings like eagles; / they will run and not grow weary, / they will walk and not be faint."

How could I write a book about surviving loss and attracting divine favour without being in the place of favour? I cannot begin to write from something I have not experienced or tasted. Our God is a merciful and loving father. Indeed, His blessings make one rich and add no sorrow. But one may wonder why God allows pain and losses amidst blessings and favour. We may not have the answers to this, but I have learnt to dig deeper into such seasons to find areas of growth and lessons to learn.

One famous passage in the Bible that relates to favour and pain is the story of Joseph, which you can find in Genesis. Joseph had dreams about how he would become great and his brothers would be bowing down to him. He had the call of God upon his life at an early age, even though the reality happened much later after so many detours. We find him thrown into a pit by his brothers and then sold to Egypt as a slave. In Egypt, he landed in Potiphar's house, where Potiphar's wife had a liking for him and wanted to sleep with him, but he refused. He stated, "How then could I do such a wicked thing and sin against God?" (Genesis 39:9). It is not that Joseph was made out of metal, neither was he very extraordinary. I believe that he was as human as can be, or as all of us are. But he chose integrity over pleasure and his personal safety.

So, as Potiphar's wife finally managed to have Joseph within her reach, she attempted to force him to lay with her, but Joseph escaped, leaving behind his garment. Potiphar's wife, now furious, schemed to lie to her husband that Joseph was trying to rape her. Usually such offences deserved a death sentence as punishment, but maybe Potiphar had some doubt about his wife's allegations. He instead demanded for Joseph to be thrown in prison.

In prison, Joseph remained for a couple of years. But Scripture says that he did not wallow himself in self pity or die in anger, depression, and disillusionment. He would have probably questioned God about why this was happening to him. What happened to all the dreams of greatness that He had given him? But Joseph was patient and the most well-behaved prisoner. He even received the job of being in charge over all the prisoners. He kept his cool amidst calamities and disaster in his life. This was not the same for the other prison inmates. We see a baker and cup bearer who were also imprisoned with Joseph looking sad and disillusioned. Joseph approached them asking why they were sad.

How we respond to the difficulties we encounter in our life's journey will determine whether we are winners or whiners in God's kingdom. Joseph turned his disappointment in prison into a divine appointment and was now serving his fellow inmates. Through the help of God, Joseph was able to interpret the dreams of these two inmates. The dreams were causing them sadness. As the dreams came to pass, one of them was released from prison and sent back to the palace while the other was beheaded. Pharaoh got to learn about Joseph's ability to interpret dreams through the inmate who was freed and was now serving in the palace. As the king also had a dream, he sent for Joseph to help interpret it after everyone else had failed to interpret it.

Eventually, Joseph was placed in charge—second in command after the king in the palace—and his dreams became a reality. Joseph's brothers thought that by selling Joseph off as a slave they were destroying him and would no longer have to bow down before him as his dreams had suggested. But as the Scripture states in Genesis 50:20, what the brothers intended for harm, God used for good to accomplish the saving of many lives in Egypt and beyond, therefore fulfilling Joseph's purpose. Your enemies may plan your destruction; they may slander you, persecute you, drag your name under the mud, and do all sorts of things to make sure you are destroyed. Like Joseph, forgive them, love them, and pray for them. They have no authority over your destiny.

What the Lord has planned for you is yours alone, and it will manifest itself at the right time. When pain and losses assail you, stay calm and stay put. You may have experienced divorce, job loss, lost a loved one through death, or are experiencing a crisis in your marriage or relationships right now. You might feel resigned to a life that is less than God's best. But hold on, hang in right there. The Lord does not waste any experience. He uses every experience that you face for your good and for His glory. Romans 8:28 (KJV) says, "And we know that all things work together for good to them that love God, to them who are the called according to his purpose." Turn your eyes to Jesus and trust Him to transform every experience for your good and for His glory.

As a mother, you may wonder how this could be true when you have lost your children through miscarriage, stillbirth, or even death. How could this be true when your husband has left you with young children to care for? There is another woman who wonders how she will be able to raise four boys on her own without a father figure. One woman struggles in her marriage with an unbelieving spouse or a troubled marriage because of other third-party interferences. Why do we have all these disappointments on our journey even though we are believers? Let me encourage you, woman of faith, that life's devastating detours often become the miraculous milestones charting a new path toward God's future for us.

Had I given up on God when I lost my job, maybe I would have been blinded to the book that He wanted me to write. This book was later picked up by a publisher in the UK—who was also a divine connection, divine favour—and is now being distributed all over the world, blessing hearts of young women. Perhaps I would not have the brand new and fulfilling job I have now had I not held on to trusting in God and clinging to His promises.

Could it be that there's a connection between the detours of life and the ultimate purpose and plan of God for our future? Scripture says in Romans 8:18 (KJV), "For I reckon that the sufferings of this present time are not worthy to be compared with the glory which shall be revealed in us." I believe that God loves to write a messy story and finish it off beautifully. Your life may be messy and full of pain, losses, and detours, but that is how the Lord loves to deal with us. I have yet to see a neat, boring story written by my God. No one enjoys watching a movie that is dull and predictable without drama. Neither does God enjoy writing the stories of our lives in a dull and predictable way.

Tamar in the Bible was a widow who disguised herself as a prostitute in order to trap her father-in-law to lay with her so she could have a child—yet we see Tamar mentioned in the lineage of a beautiful story, the Messiah. Rahab was a prostitute. Her story is in the midst of Christ's lineage. And what about Ruth, a Moabitess, an outcast, a widow? Her story ended beautifully. What about Mary the mother of Jesus? She was accused of teenage pregnancy and being an unwed mother, yet she was chosen by God to write beautifully the story of the Messiah to be born, who would bring hope and redeem the world.

Consider the story of Elizabeth; she experienced great disappointment in her life of barrenness. She waited for a long time for a child to be born who would be the forerunner of the Messiah. Probably she had many questions to ask the Lord. First, the Bible says that Elizabeth and Zechariah, her husband, were righteous and walked blamelessly in the sight of God. So, they had not sinned, and barrenness was not a punishment for their sin. Sometimes we believe that pain and loss are a result of sin or bad things that we have done; while they are in some cases, it is not always the case.

When the angel Gabriel appeared to inform Zechariah that their prayers were answered and they would have a child, he asked questions, too—they were already very old. Because of his unbelief, he was struck dumb and would remain so until the child was born. Meanwhile, Elizabeth became pregnant and glorified the Lord for the favour He had shown her. Even in our times of trouble, amidst our pain and discouragement, if we hold on, our day of favour will come. Finally, Elizabeth's child was born, and he was named John and later would be known as John the Baptist, who would prepare the way for the Messiah. He grew strong in the spirit and lived in the wilderness. Elizabeth's pain continued: she not only had to wait a long time for a son but also had to endure watching her only son live in the wilderness.

The hardships we face are not to be dismissed. We are to endure them in order to fulfill the ministry the Lord has called us to…for Jesus, it was the cross; for John the Baptist, it was a life of pain and hardships in the wilderness and finally beheading; for Elizabeth, it was the long waiting for her child. Many times, we don't get to choose the circumstances that we find ourselves in. However, we can choose how we respond to them. Whether we want our life to be for our comfort only or for the glory of God is a choice we must make. Choosing to live for the glory of the Lord attracts divine favour upon our lives. The Lord is more interested in our spiritual growth than He is in our personal comfort.

IT REALLY IS NOT THE END.

When my marriage fell apart, I tried everything humanly possible to fix my heart and clean the mess my marital breakdown presented. I felt as if my life was coming to an end when none of those things I tried worked. Going after a series of relationships, marriage counselling, emotional therapy, suicidal thoughts, and alcohol did not work. But when I raised my hands in surrender to a higher power and asked the Lord to order my life and clean my mess, then the transformation began. My heart was healed slowly but surely, and my marriage was restored miraculously. Of course, this took a lot of soul searching and submitting to God, the master healer. I sought Him deeper. In desperation, I asked Him to allow me to see my life as He saw it.

When things fall apart, it really is not the end; favour and blessings await you if you would only see things the way God sees them.

I deeply wanted to know His will for my life in the area of marriage. In intense prayers and fasting, He spoke to me in my spirit with a word that my marriage would be restored. What followed a few months later was my husband seeking a reconciliation, and because I knew this was engineered by God, I accepted, and brand-new life was given to our marriage. I have no other better term to refer to this than just the favour of God and His blessings to a desperate, erring child. You too can receive hope, healing, restoration, and transformation in whatever difficult circumstances you are going through. The Lord is not a respecter of persons but a respecter of faith. If He did it for me, He can do it for you. Only trust Him and believe.

What did not work for me in my difficult circumstances was holding on to control. Many times, when we experience pain and loss, we think that we are strong enough, smart enough, or clever enough to handle it. We think that money can solve our problems, so we work harder and harder. Or we think that having another relationship quickly will cover up our wounds. Or that alcohol and sex will help us cure our pain. But these things are only temporary solutions that numb the pain.

We must be able to get to the bottom of our core, find out the root cause of the hurt or pain, and then address it from the core. Most of the time, it is issues of anger, resentment, unforgiveness, bitterness, confusion, or insecurities rooted deep down in our core that need to be addressed for us to experience complete healing and transformation. Because of the great controversy and spiritual warfare, the enemy is crafty enough to use these things as strongholds in our lives. He causes us to fear, doubt, and develop low self-esteem, distracting us from our higher calling and God's purpose for our lives. We must stay vigilant and sensitive enough to recognize symptoms of the enemy's strongholds so that we can fight them with spiritual weapons: through prayer and the word of God.

Chapter Two:

IS THIS FAIR?

He wants to refine you just like gold so that you can be the beautiful vessel He wants you to be—fit for His holy use.

As I continued working at my new job, I enjoyed sharing the amazing love of God, His miraculous healing power, and His sufficient grace with every parent who came to the office to pay fees or interact with me for other reasons. I shared with them my experience and encouraged them to trust in the Lord more. It became apparent that my life was filled with joy, fulfillment, hope, peace, and gratitude. I could not keep it inside. I felt like the woman at the well who went to call all her neighbours to come and see this Jesus who had transformed her life.

By this time, my little princess Jess was growing in the womb and about to be born. My pregnancy was one of the easy ones. I was always overwhelmed by the mercies, grace, and favour of God upon my life in this season. As I had looked back on the divorce that had shuttered my life, I had never envisioned myself ever laughing again and enjoying every moment of my life, but here I was. The Lord had favoured me; He had established, restored, and strengthened me. See 1 Peter 5:10: "And the God of all grace, who called you to his eternal glory in Christ, after you have suffered a little while, will himself restore you and make you strong, firm and steadfast."

Sometimes I got worried and told myself not to have too much fun because my down moment was coming. But I trusted in Him who had restored me, that He would continue to put a hedge of protection around my family and me. He reminded me that if I continued to trust in Him, nothing would face me that was beyond my capacity to handle. What God had placed in my core since birth was finally beginning to flourish.

You too can experience joy, hope, peace, and contentment at the master's feet. He can restore, establish, and strengthen you in His time. You must remember to fix your eyes on Him, the author and finisher of our faith (Hebrews 12:2). He is in the business of healing, renewing, and strengthening His weary ones. Your troubles, pain, and losses do not have to overwhelm you. He has noticed your cries in trying to get out of that bad relationship. He has seen the poverty that you are experiencing, He has seen the dryness of your ministry, He has seen the sickness you are battling with. He is working on something great to be birthed out of you. Don't miss your growth opportunity during your pain and loss. Don't miss what God may be doing amid the gutters and darkness.

Isaiah 54:1-5 says:

*"Sing, barren woman,
you who never bore a child;
burst into song, shout for joy,
you who were never in labor;
because more are the children of the desolate woman
than of her who has a husband," says the* L<small>ORD</small>.

*"Enlarge the place of your tent,
stretch your tent curtains wide,
do not hold back;
lengthen your cords,
strengthen your stakes.
For you will spread out to the right and to the left;
your descendants will dispossess nations
and settle in their desolate cities.*

*"Do not be afraid; you will not be put to shame.
Do not fear disgrace; you will not be humiliated.
You will forget the shame of your youth
and remember no more the reproach of your widowhood.
For your Maker is your husband—
the* L<small>ORD</small> *Almighty is his name—
the Holy One of Israel is your Redeemer;
he is called the God of all the earth."*

Live a life of expectancy for favour, and favour will show up. Do not despair. I know what you are thinking right now—that I have no idea how deeply pained you are by your circumstances, your pain and losses. I understand, because I was in your position and nothing anybody told me made sense. But I pray that you will linger for moment and consider this: If God moved heaven and earth to restore my marriage after being divorced for six years, if He saw me through the challenges of being a single mom for the entire six years and blessed me with another child, surely, He can do the same and more for you.

One thing I would like you to remember, though: He may not answer your prayers the same way He answered mine. He knows how each one of us is formed, and He knows exactly what each of our specific needs are, so He will meet you at your very point of need. One important lesson I also gleaned through my pain and loss is that when we refuse to learn the lesson that He wants us to learn, when we fail the test that He is putting us through, He keeps cycling us back until we pass it. Why? Because He is refining us so that at the end of it, we may be as pure as gold. Don't resist the test. Pass it with flying colours by surrendering and allowing Him to fix and heal you the best way He knows how.

Consider Job of old. He was blameless and upright. A man who walked faithfully in the sight of God. He was always careful not to do evil, to the extent that he would make sacrifices on behalf of his children just in case they had sinned against God. The Lord was proud of him, and when the devil came to accuse God's children, the Lord asked Satan if he had noticed His servant Job. But Satan claimed that it was because the Lord had given him wealth and good health that Job was serving Him faithfully. Over time, God allowed Satan to take away Job's wealth and touch his body but not to take away his soul.

As Satan took away, one by one, the possessions that Job had as well as his children, Job remained even stronger in trusting the Lord. In fact, his wife and friends ridiculed him and asked him to curse this God who failed to protect him from calamity. Job's trust in God remained intact despite painful sores all over his body and losing all his possessions and his children. He stated in Job 23:10, "He knows the way that I take; / when he has tested me, I will come forth as gold."

Such great faith, from Job, the man of God; who of us will trust the Lord beyond the shadow of a doubt and state such words? Sometimes the Lord allows us to go through pain and loss to test our faith. The Lord wants to use us as His trophy to show off to the world and to the enemy. He wants to confirm that He can depend on you for the next level that He wants to take you to. Will your faith remain intact amidst the storms of life?

As Satan went again to present his accusations before the master, the Lord reminded him how Job was still faithful regardless of what was taken away. Later in Job 42:10, Scripture states that Job's possessions were restored to twice as much as he had before.

In your pain and loss, will you remain faithful like Job? Or will you curse God? Will you be able to say (similar to Job's words in 1:21), "Naked I was born from my mother's womb, and naked I shall return. Let the name of the Lord be praised"? Can you confidently say, "The Lord gives, and the Lord has taken, glory be to his name"?

Judith MacFarland, a preacher of the gospel based in the Cayman Islands, once shared with us this testimony that moved me immensely. Her son faced a near-death experience but was miraculously delivered. It was not the deliverance alone that was miraculous but also the circumstances surrounding it. Judith was facing a financial crisis in her life. Money was scarce; bills were numerous. Two of her cars were damaged and needed repairs, and her children's school fees were due. She had just started a brand-new job, but no salary had been paid yet. As the calamities kept coming, she remembered having promised God that her love for Him was real, that no matter what difficulties she faced, like a job, she would be able to say, "The Lord gives and the Lord has taken—glory be to His name."

She was determined that nothing could separate her from the love of God. Schools were about to open. Her son needed money to pay fees before he could be enrolled. As her last option, she decided to approach her employer to request a salary advance so that she could send it to her son for school fees. Thankfully, her employer agreed and gave her a salary advance. Judith sent this money by Western Union money transfer and asked her son to withdraw it and pay the school fees.

Once the son got word about the money, he and his friend took the trip to the Western Union to withdraw. Unfortunately, some thugs took notice of them and followed the boys to the Western Union place. As soon as the money was withdrawn, the thugs got hold of the boys; Judith's son's friend escaped while Judith's son was beaten, and all the money taken away. The thugs also stole his cell phone, which they used to call Judith. They demanded a ransom of $750,000 in exchange for her son's freedom, since they now held him captive. Judith, filled with sorrow and desperation, called the police quickly to alert them of what was going on. She contacted two major police stations in town, which immediately started investigating the ordeal.

Thankfully, the police were able to trace and recover Judith's son, but the money was gone. The following day, this same son took the car and left home hurriedly. He was cruising down the highway speedily to search for the thugs who had stolen his money. He had said nothing to his mom. As Judith was having her usual morning prayers, she sensed great fear, as if something terrible was about to happen. As she prayed, she felt in her spirit that her son's life was in danger. So, in her prayers, she argued her case with God. "You have allowed a wicked man to live 80-plus years, and he still died without repentance," she said. "You cannot take my 21-year-old son's life now; he is not ready. And if you do take him, God, I want You to promise me that I will see him in heaven," she continued.

As she continued in this prayer, she felt the devil reminding her to state her promise that the Lord gives, and the Lord takes; glory be to His name. "Say it now," the devil implored her. She shakily began to state, "The Lord gives and……" She could not finish her statement. She paused for a bit and then repeated her prayer to the Lord. "God, if you are taking him now, make sure that I see him on the resurrection morning." Then she continued to state her promise, "The Lord gives, and He has taken; glory be to His name."

Meanwhile, the son skidded off the road, as his speed was extremely high, and hit a tree that was by the roadside. The crash was so bad that the entire car was a total wreck. As usual, the police arrived at the accident scene shortly after. They searched for the driver and couldn't see anyone at the driver's seat. They concluded that the driver had been thrown out through the window and crashed into the nearby bushes. One policeman went over to the back seat to investigate the damage; lo and behold, the 21-year-old boy was tucked under the back seat in a pool of blood, but he was still alive. They rushed him to the hospital and all the necessary care and treatment was given him.

Judith was called to the hospital and alerted to what had happened. To her utmost relief, her son was still alive. On recovery, he went ahead to explain how sorry he was. And that he was heading out to search for the thieves so he could recover the money. He was embarrassed to lose the money considering his mom's current financial crisis. He continued to say that before the accident, he felt as if an individual lifted him up and carried him to the back seat but the rest of it was a blur. Judith concluded that an angel commissioned by the Lord had come to rescue her son from death. They praised and glorified God for the rescue from death.

It is stories like this that confirm repeatedly the Lord's mercies and faithfulness to His dear ones. His arm is not too short to save us, nor His ear deaf that He cannot hear us. Seeing what I have become now in faith, I have no iota of regret for all the pain and losses I experienced. The six years of divorce, losing my employment at various prestigious companies because of depression and brokenness, remarrying my original husband. Yes, in addition to the job that I lost in chapter one, I had previously lost my opportunities as auditor with PricewaterhouseCoopers audit firm and Regional Municipality of Wood Buffalo. Both were rewarding careers with bright futures for growth and advancement. Satan ensured that I was shattered enough, depressed, discouraged, and broken to the point of not being able to function at work. But God remembered me. He transformed me into the masterpiece that I am today. Unshakeable, unstoppable, and unchangeable in His kingdom business. He reconnected me with the heavenly vision—God's call on my life. All these have tied together perfectly to God's will and purpose for my life. How God used these experiences to mold me and ground me has been quite a paradox.

The same is true for you. Know that God is working even in the gutters and dark places of your life, to bring out the masterpiece that you are. He wants to show you the favour that you deserve. He does not waste any experience. He is using your pain and loss to mold you. He wants to refine you just like gold so that you can be the beautiful vessel He wants you to be—fit for His holy use.

STAGES OF GRIEF

Before I conclude this chapter, I would like to discuss the phases of grief that you may experience whenever you go through pain and loss. Some people experience all five, while others experience three or four of them. Grieving is a process of recovering from loss that must not be overlooked. Take the time you need. Some people take a few months while others may take years to grieve. However long it takes, it must be allowed to happen and not be suppressed. You may remain in one of the stages for a long time or skip others entirely.

Stage 1: Denial

Grief is an overwhelming emotion. You will find yourself being in denial that the loss really happened. This mechanism is a common defence that helps numb you to the intensity of the situation. Some of the reactions in the denial stage include:

Divorce: "They are just upset; this will be over tomorrow."

Job loss: "They were mistaken; they will look for me tomorrow."

Death of a loved one: "She's not gone."

Terminal illness diagnosis: "This isn't happening to me; the results are wrong."

As you move out of this stage, the emotions you have been hiding will begin to rise. You start to be confronted with a lot of sorrow.

Stage 2: Anger

While denial is a defence coping mechanism, anger has a masking effect. The anger may be redirected to other people or inanimate objects. Anger will lead you to bitterness and resentment. Some reactions in the anger stage include: "I hate him! He will regret leaving me." "They are terrible bosses; I hope they fail." "Where is God? How dare God let this happen to me?" As the anger subsides, you begin to think more rationally.

Stage 3: Bargaining

In this stage, you may find yourself creating a lot of "what if" and "if only" statements. Many people try to make a deal or promise to God in return for healing or relief from the grief and pain. Bargaining helps you postpone the sadness, confusion, or hurt.

Stage 4: Depression

Depression may feel like a quiet stage of grief. You may find yourself isolating from others in order to fully cope with the loss. Depression can be difficult and messy. It can feel overwhelming. You may feel foggy, heavy, and confused. Your reactions in this stage may be: "Why go on at all?" "I don't know how to go forward from here." "What am I without her?" "My whole life comes to this terrible end."

Stage 5: Acceptance

This is not necessarily a happy or uplifting stage of grief. It doesn't mean you have moved past the grief or loss. However, it means that you have accepted it and have come to understand what it means in your life now. Look to acceptance as a way to see that there may be more good days than bad, but there may still be bad—and that's ok. Some reactions to acceptance include: Divorce: "Ultimately, this was a healthy choice for me." Job loss: "I'll be able to find a way forward from here and can start a new path."

Death of a loved one: "I am so fortunate to have had so many wonderful years with him, and he will always be in my memories."

Terminal illness diagnosis: "I have the opportunity to tie things up and make sure I get to do what I want in these final weeks and months."

Chapter Three:

WHOM HE LOVES HE PRUNES

> *Character cannot be developed in ease and quiet. Only through experience of trial and suffering can the soul be strengthened, ambition inspired, and success achieved.*
> — Helen Keller

Noella is happily married and a mother of two girls. She is also a devoted Christian. I met with her at a birthday party where our children were invited, and we were discussing life and the blasting of life. We talked about children, spouses, and so forth. But then a touchy topic came up and Noella did not want to go there…She had suffered the loss of two children. One through stillbirth, and the other through miscarriage. Her main question was why the Lord allows so much suffering, yet He is a loving father. She had heard about my book *Broken but Blessed* and wanted to read it, but she had hesitated because she said that her wounds were still fresh. She did not want to read any material that would remind her of her own brokenness. I finally convinced her to get a copy of the book and read it. I hope that she found relatable experiences in my book that could help her navigate through her own pain and loss. Her main dilemma was that she did not understand why a loving God would allow anyone to go through such deep anguish and pain.

This is the case with many of us. We wonder why a good God would allow so much pain and suffering. I have seen many dedicated servants of God enduring so much pain and suffering. Some are well-to-do gospel music ministers who are struggling to have children after long periods of marriage. Others have gone through domestic violence and left their marriages. Others are struggling to meet the right partner to marry while others have lost their beloved children or spouses through death…and the list goes on. Why does the Lord seem to withhold good things from those who love Him and serve Him diligently?

Could it be pruning that is happening? Proverbs 3:11-12 says, "My son, do not despise the Lord's discipline, / and do not resent his rebuke, / because the Lord disciplines those he loves, / as a father the son he delights in."

John 15:2 also says, "He cuts off every branch in me that bears no fruit, while every branch that does bear fruit, he prunes so that it will be even more fruitful."

Could it also be that shaking is happening so that whatever needs to be shaken is being shaken? And what remains is what can no longer be shaken? As Hebrews 12:28-29 says, "Therefore, since we are receiving a kingdom that cannot be shaken, let us be thankful, and so worship God acceptably with reverence and awe, for our 'God is a consuming fire.'"

So, don't be afraid. The enemy wants to get you distracted and try to draw you into fear, panic, and anger. God is releasing perfect peace and love that will change the spiritual atmosphere around you. This is not a time to regress or protest. Instead, it is a time to reset and come into agreement with heaven and resist the attacks of the enemy.

First Peter 4:12-19 tells us,

> "Dear friends, do not be surprised at the fiery ordeal that has come on you to test you, as though something strange were happening to you. But rejoice inasmuch as you participate in the sufferings of Christ, so that you may be overjoyed when his glory is revealed. If you are insulted because of the name of Christ, you are blessed, for the Spirit of glory and of God rests on you. If you suffer, it should not be as a murderer or thief or any other kind of criminal, or even as a meddler. However, if you suffer as a Christian, do not be ashamed, but praise God that you bear that name. For it is time for judgment to begin with God's household; and if it begins with us, what will the outcome be for those who do not obey the gospel of God? And,

"If it is hard for the righteous to be saved,

what will become of the ungodly and the sinner?"

So then, those who suffer according to God's will should commit themselves to their faithful Creator and continue to do good."

Friends, if God allows you to go through suffering, He has a good reason for it. Sometimes He wants to break our strong-willed, disobedient nature and bring us to alignment with His nature. He wants to cause us to mature and conform more to His image. He wants to reveal to us His will for our lives and give us the opportunity to grow in righteousness.

When the Lord allowed me to go through my own breaking, I resisted Him several times. I thought that I was strong and capable of handling my own life. So, I worked harder, made more money, ensured that I had the most fun with my life through some not-so-good indulgence. But the more I resisted the breaking, the more my life spiralled downward until at one point I was too low to pick myself up. Now I realize that He wanted me to be in this position so that He could pick me up, clean me up, and use me for His purposes. Friend, when we resist the pruning, the breaking, the shaking, or the crushing that the Lord will sometimes allow us to go through, we only invite more trouble because He will keep cycling us back until we learn what He wants to teach us.

Trust in the Lord without an iota of unbelief and watch Him turn all your life's blasting into blessings. He will also turn all your trials into a triumphant song. He is always at work behind the scenes divinely orchestrating events to bring about His purposes in our lives. Stay focused on Him, beloved.

The only remedy for our broken spirit is surrendering to the Father. It is in looking to Him that we will ultimately find the greatest hope, joy, peace, and freedom. Regardless of what circumstances we face, our loving Father is there to guide us, protect us, and provide for us perfectly. When we come to the crossroads of life and we do not know which way to turn, our ears will hear His voice behind us saying, "This is the way; walk in it" (Isaiah 30:21). So, today release all the pain you feel into His care and learn to rest in Him. Say, "Lord, I surrender all. Heal my broken spirit and increase my faith."

What if you have certain life expectations that are not being met? What if you have unfulfilled deep longings in your heart? What do we do when our desires are not met in our timelines? It is normal to feel restless and frustrated. But Christ says, "I am the vine; you are the branches. If you remain in me and I in you, you will bear much fruit; apart from me you can do nothing…If you remain in me and my words remain in you, ask whatever you wish, and it will be done for you" (John 15:5, 7).

What if we have abided with Him with no positive results? Hold on to the abiding life. Rest in Him, trust in Him, and draw from Him everything that you need.

Here are more words of wisdom from the Word of God regarding trials and testing:

> Consider it pure joy, my brothers and sisters, whenever you face trials of many kinds, because you know that the testing of your faith produces perseverance. Let perseverance finish its work so that you may be mature and complete, not lacking anything. If any of you lacks wisdom, you should ask God, who gives generously to all without finding fault, and it will be given to you. But when you ask, you must believe and not doubt, because the one who doubts is like a wave of the sea, blown and tossed by the wind. That person should not expect to receive anything from the Lord. Such a person is double-minded and unstable in all they do. (James 1:2-8)

David understood adversity very well. After being anointed king, he was sought by the jealous King Saul and hunted like an animal. He experienced terrible battles and losses and suffered heartbreaks that would send the strongest soul into despair. Yet through it all, he wrote: "Preserve me, oh God: for in thee do I put my trust" (Psalm 16:1 KJV). David's experience repeatedly gives us evidence that in times of trials and adversity, the best course of action is always to seek God more, not less.

Consider the pain and suffering that Jesus Christ our Lord Himself experienced. The events leading up to His death were horrific. We see Him in the garden of Gethsemane crying tears and His sweat was mixed with blood in sorrow and pain. He even asked the Lord to let the cup of suffering pass Him by if it was His will. But the Son of Man had to suffer for us to be redeemed. His blood had to be shed as an atonement for our sin. He was a man of many sorrows. He had nowhere to lay His head. His own family rejected Him. Many times, we see Him hiding away from His own city to avoid the enemies who were hunting Him down.

But He did not give up His mission to save mankind. He bore His pain all the way to the cruel cross of Calvary. He longed for His loved ones to be with Him through this hard time. James, Peter and John—He longed for their support and comfort because He was 100 percent human as well as 100 percent divine. But the disciples had probably not understood the intensity of the pain that Jesus was going through. They were busy sleeping when Jesus wanted them to watch and pray with Him only for one hour.

You see, your friends, family, or loved ones may not exactly understand your struggles. They may not see your losses or your pain the way you see them. So sometimes it is useless to keep discussing it with them. Though they may sympathize and empathize, they still will not understand exactly how you feel. I am always comforted when I remember that Jesus understands exactly how I feel. He knows how deep the pain and hurt are. And He knows what to do to bring healing and restoration. If I trust Him and trust His process, I will be okay. I would like you to also understand this.

To wrap up this chapter, I would like to share with you five points to remember whenever you suffer loss:

1. Clinging to the Lord in brokenness is the key to wholeness:

   Seek God's face in your brokenness. Pursue Him deeper. Fast and pray so that He carries you through it and reveals to you the purpose for your pain.

2. Everything you lose the Lord will cause to be restored:

   In His own time according to His will, He makes all things beautiful. Trust Him. First

Peter 5:10 says that after you have suffered for a little while, God will strengthen you, restore you, and establish you.

3. The Lord is the Master Healer:

   When your heart is broken, take it back to Him—the manufacturer. He alone can mend your heart the best way He sees fit, so surrender your heart to Him. He will mold you back as He intended you to be. He will turn your sadness into dancing. He will give you an oil of joy instead of mourning and a crown of beauty instead of ashes (Isaiah 61:3).

4. God is in control over the most adverse of circumstances:

   Embrace every circumstance that God sends or allows; even go as far as to consider it pure joy in the hope that God's ultimate purpose will be fulfilled. (See James 1:2.)

5. For every pain, there's a purpose:

   Patiently persevere until the purpose of your pain is revealed. You will discover that everything has worked out together for your good and for His glory. (See Romans 8:28.)

PART I WORKBOOK AND SELF-ASSESSMENT QUESTIONS

1. What was your first reaction to your unexpected pain or loss?

2. What triggered your reaction?

3. How did you process this pain or loss at the 1/3/6 months phase?

4. How about at the 2/4/6-year mark? How did you process the pain or loss?

5. Did anyone support you through your pain or loss?

6. What activities did you engage in during this time?

7. How did your life change as a result of the pain or loss?

8. Which stages of grief did you experience?

9. What has helped you to accept the loss and heal from the pain?

10. What section of Part I is relatable to your experience of pain and loss

PART II:

HOW TO ATTRACT DIVINE FAVOUR

Chapter Four:

KEYS TO ATTRACT DIVINE FAVOUR

Psalm 5:12: Surely, Lord, you bless the righteous; you surround them with favor as with a shield.

Before I finally solved the puzzle of how to attract favour for every season of my life, I used to show up in a room and opportunities would just slip me by. Other people and other ideas would get preference over mine. In job interviews, other applicants would get qualified over me. In relationships, other friends would get favoured over me. But when I discovered how to attract favour, my journey took a different trajectory. Now favour is my language. When I show up at a door, it swings open before I knock. When I am at a board room, decisions are made in my favour. Everywhere I go, favour follows me.

Favour is a noun that refers to the support or approval of something or someone. Divine favour, therefore, is God's support or approval of someone. It is God's good face (Numbers 6:25-26). It is the support of the almighty God. Proverbs 16:15 (KJV) says, "In the light of the king's countenance is life; and his favour is as a cloud of the latter rain." Divine favour denotes divine preference where God prefers you to others. It also means the mercy of the almighty God. You can see it in these examples.

Psalm 44:3 (KJV): "For they got not the land in possession by their own sword, neither did their own arm save them: but thy right hand, and thine arm, and the light of thy countenance, because thou hadst a favour unto them."

Psalm 30:5: "For his anger lasts only a moment,
but his favor lasts a lifetime;
weeping may stay for the night,
but rejoicing comes in the morning."

Psalm 5:12: "Surely, Lord, you bless the righteous; you surround them with favor as with a shield."

Proverbs 12:2: "Good people will obtain favor from the Lord."

Favour is God's powerful presence on your life. Favour is what opens doors that no man can shut. Favour is what puts you in positions that nobody thinks you are qualified for. Favour is what enables you to do things that you know are beyond your capacity, but God has placed you and positioned you and prepared a way for you in order to do them. Divine favour is what causes you to sit in rooms you would have otherwise never sat in. It is what causes you to be noticed by people who would have never noticed you. Divine favour brings you recognition from people who otherwise would reject you. Divine favour causes your name to be known and called in high places.

If you have the Holy Spirit of God, you have favour, and that is all of us when we accept Jesus and are baptised in Him. There's only one thing that invites the powerful presence of the Lord in our lives, hence attracting favour consistently: holiness. You must decide to lay aside every sin and everything that easily entangles you so that you can run with endurance the race that has been set before you (Hebrews 12:1).

Favour is attracted to the real version of you that was created. When you take your position as a child of God, co-heir of God's kingdom with our brother Jesus, and pursue the kingdom (the reign and rule of God Himself) with the authority given you, blessings and favour become add-ons. The Lord is looking for people who are sold out for the kingdom business so that He can trust them with riches, influence, and favour.

I am writing this book to help someone attract the same favour upon their lives. If you struggle with things and people always working against you, here is your solution. Join me in this journey as you continue to read along.

Some of the characteristics I have observed of those who experience the favourable hand of God poured into their lives are:

1. Purpose:

Those who attract divine favour upon them consistently live purpose-driven lives. They search for their purpose and pursue it with intentionality. They do not procrastinate, and they do not allow laziness or fear to stop them from pursuing their purpose.

2. Prayer:

Prayer is power. A woman of prayer is a powerful woman. Prayer is the key to the heavenly riches, the key to divine guidance, and certainly the key to unlock divine favour.

3. Faith:

Without faith, fear prevails. Fear works against everything that purpose and prayer try to achieve. When you doubt and live in unbelief, you cannot attract favour.

4. Obedience:

Walking obediently and uprightly attracts favour in every season. The Lord is always proud of, always supports, and always approves of a servant who walks obediently and in alignment to His Word and statutes. Look at Job: The Lord was proud of him and he walked uprightly. Look at Enoch: he walked obediently, and the Lord lifted him up to heaven so he never tasted death. I usually live by this principle: obey God and leave the consequences to Him.

5. Industrious:

Favour follows you when you put your best efforts into achieving a desired goal. Heaven's resources back up someone who shows commitment and works hard. Even in ministry, there is a certain amount of human effort that we must put in with which God can work to multiply and bless us.

6. Co-operative:

When we cooperate with the Lord, He establishes us. There's a passage of Scripture that says to commit your plans unto the Lord and he will establish them (Proverbs

16:3). We must be willing to allow Him to take the lead even in our own plans. I usually pray that God would cancel every plan of mine that would lead me to destruction and establish every plan that would help me walk in His will for my life. I always pray that God would protect me even from myself because I am incapable of making any good decisions without Him. He answers this prayer.

7. Praise:

The Lord inhabits our praises. Our lives are empowered through our praises. When praises go up, blessings come down and miracles come down. Remember Paul and Silas in prison: even in chains, surrounded by prison guards and behind closed doors, they manifested a spirit of praise. They prayed and praised the Lord, and in the midnight hour, the Lord was so pleased with them that He thundered from heaven and broke loose the chains, broke open the prison doors, and freed them (Acts 16). Now I will discuss ten keys for your consideration as to how you can begin to attract divine favour consistently. Keep reading on….

1. Right Standing with God:

Psalm 5:12 (KJV): "For thou, LORD, wilt bless the righteous; with favour wilt thou compass him as with a shield."

Isaiah 3:10 (KJV): "Say ye to the righteous, that it shall be well with him: for they shall eat the fruit of their doings."

Psalm 34:10: "Those who seek the Lord lack no good thing."

There you have it directly from the Word of God. Having a right standing with Him will guarantee divine favour following you. Being righteous doesn't mean being perfect, it means seeking after the heart of God. It means seeking to please Him first and best in everything we do.

2. Consistent Earnest Expectation:

Expectation is a strong belief that something will happen in the future. Psalm 9:18 (KJV) says, "For the needy shall not always be forgotten: the expectation of the poor shall not perish for ever." What you don't expect, you don't receive. Wake up every day expecting favour, and favour will show up.

Paul also modeled this, as he wrote in Philippians 1:20 (KJV): "According to my earnest expectation and my hope, that in nothing I shall be ashamed, but that with all boldness, as always, so now also Christ shall be magnified in my body, whether it be by life, or by death."

3. Love for God and His church:

The more you love God and pursue Him, the more He responds to you with favour. When we honour Him, He will honour us. David honoured God so much that God kept overlooking his faults. He was the man after God's own heart.

Love God and love the church by winning souls for Him consistently. Always allow God's business to take first place in your life. Other examples in Scripture include 1 Kings 3:3, 1 Corinthians 2:9, 1 Chronicles 28:4, and Matthew 6:33.

From my own personal journey, I have learnt that the more I pursue God, the clearer I hear from Him speaking through dreams, turning circumstances around in answer to my questions, or even directly leading me to hear Him as I read His Word or pray.

One time, I had a deep need to hear God's direction regarding a decision that I needed to make. That day, I was keen in my spirit, saying continuous prayers in my heart. I even skipped my breakfast and lunch meals because I was hungry to hear from Him. My prayer was, "I am pursuing you deeper, oh Lord, answer me." Amazingly, that night, I saw in a dream the answer to my question, and I was peaceful. Love God and pursue Him deeper in your situation; He will answer you because He is a merciful and faithful God.

4. Humility:

If you are not humble, you cannot be favoured. The Lord resists the proud but gives grace to the humble (James 4:6). Also, Scripture says to humble yourself in the sight of God and in due course, He will lift you up (James 4:10). Another reference is 1 Peter 5:6: "Humble yourselves, therefore, under God's mighty hand, that he may lift you up in due time."

Always remain small in your own eyes. Behaving bigger than you are is the fastest way to be made smaller than you are. I find that humility is something that we must intentionally work on. Our human nature is mostly inclined to pride. But when we die daily to self and allow Christ to live in us and through us, we can remain humble as we follow Christ's example. When He was on earth, He ate with the poor, visited with the less fortunate, and mixed with all people, whether Jews or Gentiles.

5: Divine Guidance:

When I am confused or unsure which way to go or the right decision to make, I purpose to seek divine guidance. Before I came to learn how important it is to seek divine guidance, I used to seek help for decision making from my parents, spouse, and friends. Sometimes they helped, but other times it became disastrous because most of the time they did not understand very well the exact details of my circumstances or exactly how I felt.

In my book *Broken but Blessed*, I discuss how I sought the Lord to guide me in a very important area of my life. As I prayed and dry fasted for three days (no water or food), my question was, "Lord, who is my destined husband?" On the last day of the fast, the Lord said to me in a spiritual prompting, "If I give you another husband, my word will be a lie." Shortly after this revelation, my marriage was restored, after six years of brokenness.

Woman of God, I encourage you to apply this principle of seeking God's guidance when faced with a dilemma or even in the small and big decisions you must make every day. Pray in faith. Fast if you will. Let the Lord guide you to the steps you must take.

Consider these Scriptures:

Psalm 23:
> The LORD is my shepherd, I lack nothing.
> He makes me lie down in green pastures,
> he leads me beside quiet waters,
> he refreshes my soul.
> He guides me along the right paths
> for his name's sake.
> Even though I walk through the darkest valley,
> I will fear no evil,

for you are with me;

your rod and your staff,

they comfort me.

You prepare a table before me

in the presence of my enemies.

You anoint my head with oil;

my cup overflows.

Surely your goodness and love will follow me

all the days of my life,

I will dwell in the house of the Lord

forever.

Psalm 34:4-10:

I sought the Lord, and he answered me;

he delivered me from all my fears.

Those who look to him are radiant;

their faces are never covered with shame.

This poor man called, and the Lord heard him;

he saved him out of all his troubles.

The angel of the Lord encamps around those who fear him,

and he delivers them.

Taste and see that the Lord is good;

blessed is the one who takes refuge in him.

Fear the Lord, you his holy people,

for those who fear him lack nothing.
The lions may grow weak and hungry,
but those who seek the LORD lack no good thing.

Psalm 37:23 (KJV):

"The steps of a good man are ordered by the Lord: and he delighteth in his way."

Remember the story of Esther in the Bible? She fasted for three days and three nights before going to the king with her request of saving her people, the Jews (Esther 4). Her request was granted because the Lord gave her favour in response to her prayer and fasting.

When we seek divine guidance for every decision, we are guaranteed of our heavenly Father's support and approval. He will engineer the circumstances of our lives toward the direction He wants us to go: favour.

6: Heavenly Vision:

"Where there is no vision, the people perish," Proverbs 29:18 (KJV) says. When you have a vision, provision follows you. When you are visionless, you will lack provision. Friends, heaven cannot give you a vision without a provision. Men and women of vision are usually favoured.

My own experience with a heavenly vision, provision, and favour happened as follows: The Lord gave me a burden in my heart to write my first book, *Broken but Blessed*. At the time, I had no job. I had just fallen out with my employer as I discussed in chapter one of this book. I had no desire to apply for a new job either. The Lord said, "It is time for you to write the book." No problem—I hit the library every day and drafted the manuscript, which I finished in about two months. "So, what next, Lord? I have no money to publish this book."

But we serve a God who never disappoints. A few days after the manuscript was done, I was in church and was led to pick up a church bulletin, where I saw an advert for a business manager position at one of our church schools. The miracle about this is that the day I saw this advert was the last day that the announcement was being run. It had been there three times already, and I had missed it. I quickly applied for the job and banked the job after much prayer and spiritually battling the enemy who threatened to steal the blessing. So, my salary would not only provide for my basic needs, but I would also use some of it to publish the book.

Now I had the book self-published: "What next, Lord?" I asked. "How do I promote it? Who are my buyers? I am not a talented speaker." The Lord had all the answers to my questions. He provided a connection with Stanborough Press in the UK, which is now the publisher of my book and is distributing it worldwide. As I had travelled back home in Kenya, I met with one of the superior staff at the publishing press. The meeting was made possible by the health and publishing director of the Adventist Book Center in the East and Central Africa Division based in Kenya, where I had randomly stopped in to see if they could stock my book.

What is your vision, beloved? What is your assignment here on the earth? When you connect with God and find your vision, favour will begin to follow you. The earth is the Lord's and the fullness thereof (Psalm 24:1). When we connect with Him through a heavenly vision, all of heaven's resources are at our disposal.

7: Right Company:

The psalmist warns us in Psalm 1 to be careful who we sit with, stand with, or talk with. Bad company corrupts good character. Show me your friends, and I will show you your character. Birds of a feather flock together. Some of the people you hang out with will help attract favour to you because they are highly favoured.

8: Power of Positive Declaration:

Favour answers your tongue. Speak favour over your life, and you will attract it. See these Scriptures: Luke 21:15, Psalm 81:10, and Mark 11:23. The favour you have is the favour you have spoken. When you declare, "I am well favoured, I am highly favoured, I have extravagant favour" and mean it, favour will be your portion. God created the whole world with words, and we also can create our own world with the words we speak.

9. Thanks-Living:

Develop an attitude of gratitude and you will attract divine favour. When I remember where the Lord has brought me from, I shed tears of joy, and I am amazed at His love for the undeserving ones like me. You could have died when you experienced that painful situation that was a consequence of a bad decision you had made, but the Lord preserved you. You could have lost so much more than the few losses you have experienced today, but the Lord saved you. You could have lost your mind in the middle of that crisis, but the Lord held you together.

Thank Him daily for what He has done for you so far. Sometimes we forget to thank Him, and we keep asking Him for more and more things in prayer. He is a good God who deserves all our worship, our praises, and our thanksgiving.

10: Be Sensitive to Agents of Favour:

In chapter six, we will discuss the agents of favour. The Lord can use anyone, including a stranger, to show you His favour. He can use anything and any situation to turn around things to your favour. Remain sensitive to circumstances and people who come your way. Do not dismiss anything or anyone without giving prayerful, careful consideration.

Chapter Five:

FAVOUR AND FAITH

Because of her faith, Ruth was favoured enough to bear the lineage of the Messiah.

Throughout my pregnancy with my second child, I was terrified about labour and delivery. My experience with my first child was not the best. My son was born after a long, painful labour. And because he was so fatigued with the long process, he developed some complications with his lungs. He had to be put in an incubator for three days after birth to help him with his breathing. As I watched my poor three-day-old baby lying helpless with a bunch of tubes across his nostrils, I could not help getting emotional. I forgot about my own exhaustion after birth and had no desire to go home to rest even if the doctors recommended it. Thankfully, he was fully healed and released to go home on day four. Remembering this ordeal got me anxious about the delivery of my second, so I always prayed that God would see me through an easier and safer delivery. One time as I earnestly prayed, I saw a vision of myself in the delivery room. Four angels were in the room also dressed in the hospital gear but watching from a distance as the delivery happened. God had answered my prayer in advance and revealed to me that His presence and those of the angels would be there as I delivered my second baby. What was also scary about it was that I had been diagnosed with a bacterial infection along the birth canal called Group B streptococcus (GBS). According to research, 25 percent of healthy adult pregnant women are carriers of this bacteria, which is tested for at week thirty-five to thirty-seven of pregnancy. Also, one in every 2,000 babies born under these circumstances will become ill.

While the doctor assured me that everything was under control and that the delivery would go okay, I was still nervous. I was given instructions to ensure that I rushed to the hospital as soon as my membranes ruptured. One Monday evening after cooking chapatis—my favourite bread, which takes two to three hours to cook—my membranes ruptured. This was five days beyond my due date. Thankfully, my husband was home with me, so we rushed to the hospital.

The routine for delivery was arranged and the process started. Two hours in, I developed a fever and began to shiver terribly. The nurses were anxious as they confessed to not have experienced a thing like this before. They called my delivery doctor to come and assess the situation. He inserted an internal camera to monitor the baby and recommended waiting a bit longer before a possible c-section if the fever continued. The shivering went on for about an hour.

As I lay there in pain and shivering, I reminded God about His promises to be with me. Did He forget me? I called on my close friends to also keep praying and battling with us in the spirit; then suddenly, the shivering stopped. Soon my baby was ready to be pushed out. The whole process from labour to delivery took about seven hours, and then we heard the first cry of our little princess. This was way shorter than my first child's labour and delivery, which took more than twenty-four hours!

The utmost relief was that my baby did not catch the fever or infection we thought would get transferred from me at birth. However, I was not allowed to cuddle her right after birth as they had to ensure my temperature was under control first. The following day at noon, we were released to go home with our bundle of joy, beautifully tucked in her brand-new outfit and blankets.

Favour showed up once more! What a beautiful blessing! Always, the enemy wants to steal our blessings. Clearly, he was present in the delivery room to wage war against my angels, to cause fear and doubt, and bring destruction. But God stood up and showed Himself strong on my behalf. As we battled in prayer and claimed His promises, He did not fail us. This baby was a complete blessing from conception to birth, and today she continues to receive gifts from friends and family. I interpret it as God's way of using my friends and family to bless us.

God will show Himself strong on your behalf if you wholeheartedly seek Him and wait patiently for Him in your situation (2 Chronicles 16:9). He is a promise keeper and way maker. He will move heaven and earth to bless you and keep you safe when you commit your ways to Him.

But we must be ready to fight the good fight. Paul writes, "For our struggle is not against flesh and blood, but against the rulers, against the authorities, against the powers of this dark world and against the spiritual forces of evil in the heavenly realms" (Ephesians 6:12). He goes on to say that we must be ready to put on the full armour of God, so that we can be able to stand firm in the day of trouble. The full armour of God includes:

The belt of truth- Know the truth for yourself from the Word of God and be obedient to it.

The breastplate of righteousness- Don't tolerate sin on a daily basis.

The gospel of peace- The Word of God gives us that peace in our hearts that surpasses all human understanding.

The shield of faith- The most powerful asset for believers is **FAITH**. The stronger your faith, the more apt you are to respond to all the Lord wants to do for you. Greater faith brings on greater things and greater favour.

The helmet of salvation- It protects us from thinking the wrong way, the worldly way.

The sword of the spirit (the Word of God)- It is the most powerful weapon we have in fighting against satanic attacks. We must apply the Word of God in our conduct, character, and conversation.

Finally, always pray in the spirit and stay connected in prayer so that you can be able to submit to God and resist the devil.

Friends, the enemy you are fighting against is not your spouse, your co-worker, or your employer. You must realize that your enemy is the devil. He may use your spouse, co-worker, an enticing secret lover, or employer to torment you or cause you to fall, but you must be vigilant and constantly on guard to defeat him at all costs. We must not debate with the enemy in our fight with him. Give him the Word of God and walk away.

Consider the story of Naomi and Ruth as recorded in Scripture. Naomi and her husband, Elimelek, were faced with a season of famine in their land, Judah. They decided to travel to the land of Moab where there was still plenty of food. They took with them their two sons, Mahlon and Kilion. When they arrived, their sons married Moabite women: Orpah and Ruth. Elimelek unfortunately died, and Naomi was widowed. In due time, both of Naomi's sons also died. In the days of the Bible, women relied on men for survival. The death of Naomi's husband and her sons must have left these three women—Ruth, Naomi, and Orpah—vulnerable and without support.

Word came along that Judah, Naomi's homeland, was no longer in famine. Naomi decided to return home. She called her daughters-in-law and let them know her decision, requesting that they stay behind in their homeland, Moab, because they were now widowed, and she had no one else to marry them. Orpah said her goodbyes, but Ruth refused to be left behind. She stated, "Where you go, I will go, and where you stay I will stay. Your people will be my people and your God my God. Where you die I will die, and there I will be buried. May the Lord deal with me, be it ever so severely, if even death separates you and me" (Ruth 1:16-17).

This is a woman displaying courage and faith in the middle of calamity. She must have realized that the call of God on her life was more important than her comfort. So, she decided to pursue her calling by following her mother-in-law, Naomi, to Judah. Later, Ruth was able to meet Boaz, who married her, and they had a son called Obed. Obed was the father of Jesse; Jesse was the father of David, the ancestor of our savior Jesus. Because of her faith, Ruth was favoured enough to bear the lineage of the Messiah.

Look at every event of your life and remember: God is at work divinely orchestrating events to bring about His purposes in your life. You see, the good, the bad, the unpleasant, the ugly, the gruesome, the painful, the highs and lows and in-betweens have shaped the fabric of who you are today. There's purpose in the detours and stumbling that we experience. Forgive yourself and forgive others who have hurt you and hindered your progress. Forgive those who have rejected you, forgive your previous mistakes and wrong choices, and choose to move along with God in the steps that He orders for you. God has never and will never give up on you. Stand in faith on the promises of God. Even during pain, suffering, loss, and misfortune that you cannot understand, the Lord is birthing out something. Trust Him.

You see, friend, you might be asking some questions right now: Once we know that a dream, a promise, or a goal is from the Lord, how do we look forward to it in a way that honours God as time goes by? It is easy to keep the faith when we don't have to wait for too long.

When God promised me in prayer that He was going to restore my marriage, I believed it with all my heart and waited patiently for it to come to pass. I shared with my roommate at the time that God was going to give me back the same husband I originally had. She laughed and told me to stop being crazy because it had been six years of divorce, for crying out loud! Thankfully, I did not have to wait for too long before God's promise was fulfilled. What if I had had to wait for a long time, maybe many months or years? Would I still have trusted God and waited for Him?

Let us glean some lessons from some men of faith discussed in the Bible. On two accounts, the Lord tested Abraham's faith and credited him as righteous and blameless because on both accounts he proved faithful. First, he was asked to leave the land of Ur and travel to a land that was unknown to him (Genesis 12). It took faith for him to obey, leave his people and possessions, and go to a land unknown to him. The Lord was able to bless him with descendants as many as the sands of the sea and many other countless blessings recorded in Scripture.

Secondly, Abraham had become old; he did not have a child and his wife, Sarah, was old, too. The Lord promised him that they would have a son who would be heir to his throne. Abraham's human nature took away his patience, and he went for Hagar to beget Ishmael, who was not in the plan of God for his life. Despite his detour from the plan of God, he was still given the promised son Isaac.

What amazed me about Abraham's story is that when the Lord asked him to go and sacrifice his only son on Mount Moriah, he took his son with him, obeying God's instruction faithfully (Genesis 22). He set out on a three-day journey to the mountain with his son. When they arrived at the foot of the mountain, Abraham tied up Isaac and laid him on the altar to be sacrificed as a burnt offering to the Lord. As he lifted the knife in the air to slaughter his son, the Lord's voice asked him to stop, and He provided a ram for sacrifice instead of his son. You see, the Lord sometimes wants to test our faith to prove if He can trust us with the next level that He wants to take us to.

Friends, when we, like Abraham, can remain obedient and submitted to the Lord, our promotion to the next level will come. Maybe the suffering or the loss that you are experiencing today is your test of faith. Will you pass it? Regardless of our own detours from the plan and purposes of God, His plan for our lives prevails. He does not change like we do. Our detours may cause delays to the achievement of God's plan, though, so why not patiently wait for God's plan A?

David could boldly say, "Those who seek the LORD lack no good thing" (Psalm 34:10). The only need we have is a "seek the Lord" need! To David, this was more than a nice theory. Because he had drawn near to the Lord as his Good Shepherd, he lacked nothing (Psalm 23:1). And he was so confident of God's ongoing favour in his life that he proclaimed, "Surely your goodness and love will follow me all the days of my life, and I will dwell in the house of the LORD forever" (v. 6).

David experienced this same kind of favour when the prophet Samuel was seeking God's direction on who Israel's next king should be (1 Samuel 16). Samuel knew the king was to be chosen from among the sons of Jesse, and so the sons were paraded before the prophet to see which one the Lord's choice was. Samuel must have been puzzled when none of the seven oldest sons met with God's approval, so he told Jesse: "The LORD has not chosen these…Are these all the sons you have?" (1 Samuel 16:10-11).

Apparently, no one had thought to invite David to this important gathering. He was the youngest son, and he was out tending his father's sheep. But while everyone else was looking at factors like age and rank, God was looking for a man after His heart…who would fulfill His purposes (Acts 13:22, 36).

Often the Lord asks us to wait patiently for the desires of our hearts, and the stronger our longings, the more quickly our patience runs out. Friends, your other question may be: if the Lord has promised to restore your loss, why has He delayed? How do you continue to honour Him until He brings it to fruition?

First, do not be discouraged: As Abraham, David, and Joseph showed, God's delays are not denials. He knows exactly what you need, the graces that must be developed in your character, what areas in your faith require growth, and what details must be arranged. He will wait until you are ready to send you the blessing.

Second, God acts on behalf of those who wait for Him (Isaiah 64:4) and He always keeps His promises (Isaiah 55:11). Give God time to accomplish His will in your life. Don't give up obeying Him. Soon enough, He will answer your prayers in ways beyond your expectations. People in the Bible were asked to do such things as dip in the Jordan River (Naaman), give their last bit of food to the prophet (the widow with Elijah), stretch out their withered hand, and wash in the Pool of Siloam. But whenever people exercised their faith and obeyed the Lord, He did miracles!

What step of faith is God asking you to take today? If you are waiting for Him to release His FAVOUR, He may be waiting for you to stretch out for it! I'm convinced that a great harvest of favour is coming to your life as you sow seeds of faith, expectancy, and obedience.

Chapter Six:

AGENTS OF FAVOUR

But those who follow Christ are ever safe under His watch care. Angels that excel in strength are sent from heaven to protect them. The wicked one cannot break though the guard which God has stationed about His people. — Ellen G. White, The Great Controversy

We were returning from visiting my folks back in the rural village where my parents were born. Traffic was bad and public transportation was scarce because everyone was returning to work and school after the holidays. After a struggle, we managed to get space in a minibus that was travelling shortly to the city where we were going. My two children, mom, and cousin were with me. As we waited for the bus to fill up, I requested Mom to get my phone charged at a nearby shop as my battery was very low. My iPhone is very dear to me because I save all my notes, music, and sermons on it. Coming up that weekend, I had a speaking engagement at a church on surviving the loss of a loved one. My sermon notes were well saved on my phone, and I was 80 percent ready to speak.

The minibus driver announced that we were ready to board, so everyone hopped into the vehicle and we would soon leave. Recall, I had my iPhone still charging at the shop; I did not remember to grab it. Just before the driver hit the gas pedal, a young lady seated at the back called up to me requesting to borrow my charger. It was at that moment we realized I had not picked up my phone from the shop. I asked my mom to jump out and grab the phone, with a tinge of fear in my heart, praying that my phone had not gone missing. Thankfully, she was able to collect it. Relieved, I stretched out to lend the lady at the back seat my charger. It did not work for her! Apparently, she had a Samsung phone and those are not compatible with iPhones for charging. Look at how God sent an angel in the form of this lady to ask for my charger so that I could realize at that point that my phone was not with me. Isn't God good?

It is events like this that constantly remind me of God's goodness and protection over his children. Ellen G. White, in the book *The Great Controversy,* states: "But those who follow Christ are ever safe under His watch care. Angels that excel in strength are sent from heaven to protect them. The wicked one cannot break though the guard which God has stationed about His people" (cited in Truth About Angels 1996, 13).

Soon after I had released my book *Broken but Blessed* as a self-published book, I travelled to Kenya to visit my family. I had a few copies of the book in boxes to give to friends and family as well as distribute to bookstores as I asked them to consider selling the book on my behalf.

As I moved around the city looking for a bookstore that would stock my book, I was amazed at how God intervened. At the Adventist Book Center, they asked me if I would like to have my book distributed all over the world. My answer was absolutely yes! So, the guy in charge at the book center gave me a phone number to the director of publishing in their organization. I made an appointment to pay him a visit. While at the publishing director's office, he mentioned that he had a friend at a UK publisher called Stanborough who was due to visit Kenya. He said he would connect me with her so that she could review my manuscript for possible publishing.

A few days later, the lady arrived in Kenya, and I was able to meet with her. She requested a couple copies of my book and spent a few days reading through. Before she left Kenya, she contacted me and said that my book was quite interesting, and she would like to partner with me in spreading its message worldwide by publishing it. I was so thrilled and thankful to God that He would provide this divine connection.

Experiences with the mysteries of God are exactly that: mysterious. He can use anybody and anything as an agent to show you His favour and to bless you.

Consider the story of Queen Esther in the book of Esther in the Bible. She was an orphan. But even after losing her parents, God provided Mordecai, her cousin, to care for her and lead her into her destiny and purpose in life. Esther was a beautiful, humble, and God-fearing young woman.

As King Xerxes desired a new wife, word was sent all over the kingdom to call upon beautiful young virgins to present themselves before the king so that he could select a new wife. These women were to be beautified with oils and perfumes for one year before they could appear before the king. As Esther came to the contest at the suggestion of Mordecai, she pleased and won favour with everyone who saw her. When the time came for her to be presented to King Xerxes, she also pleased him and won his favour over everyone else who had been presented. Esther was crowned queen over Vashti.

Now it came a time when the Jews faced a challenge to their survival. Esther, who was raised as a displaced, orphaned Jewess raised by her relative, was informed by Mordecai's sources that the Jewish people were scheduled for extinction by the wicked Haman, the vice regent second in command only to King Xerxes. As she received the news, Esther advised Mordecai to gather all the Jews for three-day and three-night prayer and fasting. They were not to eat or drink anything for those three days, after which Esther would approach the king with a request to free the Jews from the wicked plan of Haman. After the fast, Esther had received wisdom and guidance from the Lord on how she would approach the king with her request.

As she went to present her request, the king was pleased and promised to grant whatever she requested. We see that Queen Esther planned a two-day banquet for the king and Haman, and on the second day, she presented her request for the king to save the Jews from destruction. The king was very furious to learn of Haman's wicked plan to destroy Esther's people. He allowed the Jews to defend themselves against attack, and Haman was impaled on a pole, while Mordecai was given the power to replace Haman in the authority of second in command to the king.

You see, Esther knew where to go in order to receive favour in everyone's eyes. She knew that by prayer and fasting, she would receive wisdom and divine guidance to navigate through her problems. This is the example that you and I must follow as we navigate through our daily challenges. We may experience pain and loss as presented by the devil and the enemies of God in the dark world. But when we hide under the shadow of the almighty God, we have sure protection, as we see in Psalm 91:1-2: "Whoever dwells in the shelter of the Most High will rest in the shadow of the Almighty. I will say of the Lord, 'He is my refuge and my fortress, my God, in whom I trust.'"

Esther was an orphan, and in today's language, she had no connections in high places. Yet we see her being highly favoured and chosen to be the queen. That makes me ponder this question, and you can think about it, too: what one thing do I have that I can capitalize on and use to impact the world for the Lord? For Esther, it was her beauty. She used her beauty to gain the favour of everyone who saw her and eventually fulfill the Lord's purpose of saving His people from the hand of the enemy.

Recall the story of Moses, who was used by the Lord to deliver the Israelites from the hand of the enemy, Pharaoh. He only had one thing in his hand: a rod that God would use in order to convince Pharaoh to let his people go. When God called Moses into this ministry through a burning-bush experience, Moses felt the least likely to be used for this purpose. He was not eloquent in speech; he was a fugitive running away from a crime he had committed back in Egypt; he was a shepherd and all that. But God used him regardless of his inadequacy. In Exodus 4:2, He simply asked him the question, "What do you have in your hand?"

The one thing that you have in your hand is all that the Lord needs to use in order to bring about a miracle in your life. Yes, you may have experienced losses and pain. You may have lost a loved one through death or divorce. You may have lost your footing in a career that you really love. You may have suffered losses in a business where you had put all your investment in. But what is that one thing that you have left in your hands? If you surrender it to God, He can multiply it and use it to favour you and generations to come.

Elijah the prophet went to Zarephath as directed by the Lord to a widow whom the Lord had appointed to provide food for Elijah. When Elijah arrived in Zarephath, he met this widow collecting sticks to go and make food for herself and her only son (see 1 Kings 17:8-14). Elijah called on this lady to give him a drink of water and a piece of bread. But the lady replied that she did not have any bread, only a handful of flour in a jar and a little olive oil in a jug to prepare a last meal for herself and her son before they ran out of food and starved. This woman had no idea that the favour of the Lord was pursuing her to bless her in the overflow. All she needed to do was to heed to the word of God spoken through Elijah that if she provided a piece of bread to Elijah, her jug of oil and jar of flour would not be used up or run dry until it rained again.

Sometimes the Lord wants us to only respond obediently to His instruction in order to attract His favour upon our lives. Sometimes He will place a burden in our hearts that will always look bigger than ourselves. It may look impossible in the now. He just requires a step of faith into it, and then He will back it up with His favour and resources in the overflow. Just like He blessed this widow in the overflow after she responded obediently to feed Elijah, the man of God.

What is it that you need to stretch out into in order to unlock and attract divine favour upon your life consistently? You may require a step of faith into a new career, a new business, a new relationship, a new ministry, or even a new mind-set. Stretch out, enlarge the tents of your dwelling. Try your new thing in faith and wait for favour to show up. You may be on your way to experiencing an overflow of peace, love, and joy in your relationships, finances, ministry, or business. Hold on to that word that God has spoken upon your life in faith. The Lord wants your life to leave footprints of His glory. When I wrote my debut book, *Broken but Blessed*, I had no idea whose life it would impact. With no resources, except my own time and limited intellect, I obeyed God's voice and put together a manuscript. Sure enough, the Lord was able to provide resources and connections for the book to be available worldwide. I prayed, and I still pray to date, that the Holy Spirit and the ministering angels will push this book and subsequent books into the hands and hearts of those whose lives I am supposed to touch.

A very heartwarming testimony is one from my friend Joyce, who wrote to me a few months after she had read my book. This is what she wrote: "Things in our marriage were extremely bad. There was communication breakdown, challenges that come with being new parents, in-laws, unmet expectations, finances, etc. My husband and I had agreed to live together until I went back to work or got my financial stability back, then he would move out. I got your book, read it, and left it on the nightstand. My husband also read it without my knowledge.

"A few days after, he came and asked me if I had read the book and whether I still wanted to go ahead with the separation plans. I did not answer, but deep down, I knew I didn't want to. We talked about prayers and how it had changed your situation. We agreed to start fellowship at our home, praying and sharing the word. It has been four months now, and our marriage has been transformed. We talk and laugh just like we did during our dating days.

"With our challenges, we seem to be finding solutions without much struggle. Even when we don't, it's not as hard as it was. Honestly, I have seen the hand of God in our marriage; we wouldn't have made it this far without Him. Thank you so much for allowing God to use you as His vessel to change and restore our marriage. God bless you. We are not there yet, however, we're making progress every day."

Adversity is not God's ultimate desire for His creation. Yet God uses adversity for two reasons: to strengthen our faith and to give us a testimony to share with the world and display His glory. Pastor Wintley Phipps shared this message in one of his sermons, and I remember his words to date. He said, "It is in the quiet crucible of your personal private sufferings that your noblest dreams are born and God's greatest gifts given in compensation for what you have been through."

Let me end this chapter with a few comforting words from Scripture that encouraged me during my time of loss:

2 Corinthians 4:8-9 (KJV): "We are troubled on every side, yet not distressed; we are perplexed, but not in despair; Persecuted, but not forsaken; cast down, but not destroyed."

This was Paul writing to the Corinthian church. Paul had endured so much suffering for the gospel of Christ, yet he remained hopeful, peaceful, and patient in his suffering. In fact, even in prison, he was able to write many books encouraging the churches, and his words still give encouragement to us today.

2 Corinthians 1:3-4: "Praise be to the God and Father of our Lord Jesus Christ, the Father of compassion and the God of all comfort, who comforts us in all our troubles, so that we can comfort those in any trouble with the comfort we ourselves receive from God."

How would I be able to comfort a sister going through divorce, depression, or discouragement if I had not gone through it myself? While it is possible to do it, it may not be effective.

As we go about our life's journeys, we have the Lord's promise that He will never leave us nor forsake us. He will always provide a way of escape from our troubles and show us His favour if we completely trust Him and entrust our lives to His able hands. He says in 1 Corinthians 10:13: "No temptation has overtaken you except what is common to mankind. And God is faithful; he will not let you be tempted beyond what you can bear. But when you are tempted, he will also provide a way out so that you can endure it."

PART II WORKBOOK AND SELF-ASSESSMENT QUESTIONS

1. How have you experienced a life of favour?

2. Which of the ten keys to attracting favour are already familiar to you? Which ones are not?

3. Do you believe that having faith attracts divine favour? How?

4. How has the Lord used friends, strangers, or family to show you favour?

5. Do you believe that those who are highly favoured have certain characteristics?

PART III:

HOW TO FIND PEACE IN THE STORM

Chapter Seven:

YOU ARE CHOSEN

No matter what you do, if God has chosen you, there's no escaping His hand. You may run from Him, but you can never hide forever.

I was driving back to Fort McMurray from Saskatchewan, Alberta, Canada. It was January 1, 2013, so the roads were deserted as people were busy celebrating New Year's. Being in the thick of winter, the snow was plenty, and the roads were slippery. On the passenger side was my friend Faith, who was riding with me. "Faith, can you jump in the driver's seat and drive? I am exhausted!" I asked. She agreed to help with the driving.

As we approached Highway 28 going into Fort McMurray, the roads were more slippery and there was a black ice patch at some point. We found ourselves skidding off the road, and as Faith tried to apply the brakes, the car skidded off the road even faster. We went around and round and finally stopped upside down with a thud into a ditch. I was trembling with fear and saying my last prayers as I envisioned death coming right at me. The wheels faced up, and we were hanging onto our seats upside down. Thankfully, we had safety belts on, so we did not get thrown off the seats or out through the windows.

The ordeal lasted about three minutes, but it felt like an eternity. Police came after being called by onlooking drivers. They assessed the accident and wrote us a report, then called a towing truck to help us out. The engine oils had spilled from the car, and the body was irreparably damaged as it had hit so hard into the ditch. How did we survive that? Faith and I kept asking the question. It could only be explained as the hand of God. We could have died in this road accident that got my car damaged beyond repair. It was a complete write-off, yet I survived without a scratch or shedding any blood.

When I remember the miracles the Lord has done to keep me alive and strong today, I am amazed! Looking back at my life, I question what good the Lord saw in me to even consider using me in ministry. I do not have the cleanest past; my weaknesses are many. I am timid; I am not even close to being a good writer or speaker or singer. I am neither popular nor anyone's favourite. Yet He says that I am the apple of His eye. Yet He keeps loving me and lifting me over and over. I have many testimonies of God's grace and mercies, answered prayers and His favour. I like to pride myself in the Lord because His awesomeness is overwhelming.

One time, I received an answer to a prayer I had been praying about for six months. What was amazing is that as I dropped off my child to day care that morning, it occurred to me that I desperately needed this prayer answered soonest. So, I got back in my car and silently prayed again. I reminded the Lord what He says, that I am the apple of His eye. I asked why He had not answered this prayer to grant me this thing, yet He had already given the same to others. I ended the prayer saying let His will be done not mine. Then as I scrolled through my phone, I randomly read a message on Instagram that said, "God is working on that thing you are worried about; take your hands off the wheel."

Relieved, I began driving to work. So, I got to my destination and began putting in some work while randomly checking my emails like I often do. Lo and behold! There was the email giving me the answer to my prayer, which had been sent at 8:33 that morning. Recalling I had repeated my prayer desperately at around

8:05 that same morning, I broke into worship and praise. What a mighty God we serve.

When our identity is hidden in Him, Christ works behind the scenes to make our lives free, fruitful, and full. Maybe you have invested in something or someone, but you have not reaped any harvest or received the returns on your investment. In fact, all you have experienced from your investment is losses. Do not be discouraged; the Lord sees you. He sees every detail of your investment, and if you will not abandon ship, He will come to your aid. He is probably wanting to use your emptiness to call you to deeper faith and a more bountiful harvest.

When you accept Jesus Christ and are baptised in Him, you have put on Christ. Your life is hidden in Him; your identity is hidden in Him also. First Peter 2:9 says that you are a royal priesthood, a chosen generation, a holy nation, and a special possession to God. I believe this with all my heart, that you are special in God's eyes. He has chosen you. He wants to favour you. He delights in loving you, walking with you, showing you the way, making you happy. He delights in having an intimate relationship with you, fellowship with you. Therefore, He gets jealous when you prioritize other things and other people over Him. Sometimes, He causes you to lose that thing or that person that has priority in your life over Him for this reason. He loves to have your attention.

UNPACKING FREEDOM, FULLNESS, AND FRUITFULNESS:

You have encountered these words a few times in this book. Now let us look closely at what I mean by these beautiful alliterative words:

Freedom: It is God's will that we are free. That is why He sent His only son, to save mankind from the bondage of sin. Christ came to rescue you and me from the sin that so easily besets us. He gave us salvation and paid for it in full by His painful death on the cross. Whenever we fall back to sin, we can run back to Him for forgiveness by claiming the shed blood of Christ on the cross.

However, the Lord is pained by habitual sin. When we sin deliberately and continuously, we grieve the Holy Spirit of God and subsequently become numb to His prompting. It is important to keep our hearts pure from deliberate/wilful sin so that God's power and purposes can be made manifest in us and through us.

The Lord wants you to be free from pain, depression, and struggles. He promises peace in the storms of life when you trust in Him. When you put your hand in His hand and allow Him to lead you through your life's journey, you can be free, and rest assured that He is in control. He does not promise a life that has no trials, but He promises that we will have a heart full of singing in the middle of our storms because He is always right there with us. Whom the Son sets free is free indeed (John 8:36). Allow yourself to enjoy your freedom in Christ.

Fullness: Jesus said these words to His disciples: "I have told you these things, so that in me you may have peace. In this world you will have trouble. But take heart! I have overcome the world" (John 16:33). And He also said, "These things have I spoken unto you, that my joy might remain in you, and that your joy might be full" (John 15:11 KJV). His disciple John wrote: "You, dear children, are from God and have overcome them, because the one who is in you is greater than the one who is in the world" (1 John 4:4).

I have used these verses to illustrate that it is Christ's plan that our joy may be full. That our peace may abide, regardless of the troubles that we will encounter on our daily journey of life. We can be full of His love, His peace, His joy, His kindness, His hope, His salvation. We can be full when we remember that the king of the universe knows the good plans that He has for us (Jeremiah 29:11).

Fruitfulness: We are to live our lives in a way that we bear fruit as followers of Christ. It is not enough that we are chosen, we must be fruitful. In the parable of the vine and the branches, Christ illustrates: a branch that does not bear fruit will be cut off. A Christian who does not bear fruits will be pruned and purged so that he may bear fruit. The way to bear fruit is to remain in Jesus. "Abide in me, and I in you. As the branch cannot bear fruit of itself, except it abide in the vine; no more can ye, except ye abide in me" (John 15:4 KJV).

What does it really mean to bear fruit? I believe it means that we are to use our time, talents, and treasures wisely to contribute to the growth of the kingdom of God. Eight years ago, when I experienced divorce, every decision I made after sent me further and further away from God. I was literally running away from Him. I did not understand why a loving God would allow me to experience such a big tragedy in my life. Why did He not stop it? Why did He allow those circumstances to play out the way they did? So, I took matters in my own hands, and I made my own choices and decisions without involving Him. I prayed, but only passively. I went to church, but only as a routine. My connection with the Lord was lost. My life continued to be empty and full of discontentment. I forgot who I was in Christ and the authority I carried as a child of God and co-heir with Christ of the heavenly kingdom and all the treasures.

Friend, no matter what you do, if God has chosen you, there's no escaping His hand. You may run from Him, but you can never hide forever. He will keep pursuing you with His love and find you out. You may reject His love when He pursues you, but He will patiently wait for you to return.

When you keep running away from Him, you will notice that He may remove His hedge of protection from around you. He may allow extenuating circumstances to persist so that you may be pushed to remember Him. This is how He deals with us in order to mature us in Him.

Jonah knew this very well, after he chose to run away from a God assignment. He was called to go to Nineveh and preach the word of God. He resisted and decided to go to Tarshish instead, fleeing from God. On his way to Tarshish in a boat, there was a heavy storm that caused the boat to almost capsize. As he watched the sailors of the ship cry out for help, he knew he was the cause of the storm, for he had disobeyed the voice of God. Also, they had cast lots and it fell on him. He asked them to throw him out and said they would be safe.

As soon as Jonah arrived in the water, there was a big whale ready to swallow him alive. He stayed in the belly of the whale for three days and three nights. There he prayed and sought the Lord and vowed to obey His voice. He was soon vomited out. Having learnt his lesson and greatly fearing the consequences of disobeying God, Jonah headed to Nineveh to proclaim the message given to him by the Lord over the city. The Ninevites were living in wickedness; the Lord was planning to destroy the city. Jonah's message was received, and the

Ninevites repented in sackcloth. The Lord spared their lives and He did not destroy them.

How are you running away from the Lord? Have you suffered pain or loss to the extent that you have given up on God's hand over your life? Have you given up on God's favour over your life? Remember that God's favour is His glory. He has chosen you, and He is still in the business of saving you and drawing you to him. He will never allow you to be lost completely. Just as He was with Jonah in the belly of the fish, He is with you even when you disobey Him. He may allow you to stay in those not-so-comfortable circumstances for a while like He allowed Jonah to stay in the belly of the fish, in order to catch your attention and get you to obey Him. Maybe if Jonah had continued to disobey God, he may have stayed longer in the belly of the fish, but Jonah repented and was remorseful over his disobedience.

The Lord allowed the fish to vomit Jonah out, and he immediately headed to where God was sending him. In your circumstances, God may be looking to redirect you to where He intends you to go. Do not resist Him. Listen to His voice and go as He sends you. It will eventually be well with your soul.

You see, losses, defeats, and disappointments are universal: everyone experiences them at one point or another. But why? Why would God allow His beloved child to experience such profound heartbreaks? In this we see one of the most vital principles of the Christian life—when God chooses to work through someone, he or she will go through the process of brokenness, in order to be molded for His purposes. The Lord uses the seemingly disastrous events of our lives to make us aware of our inadequacy and to help us depend upon Him completely. So, do not despair; persevere through your losses and defeats; and remember that all things are working together for your good and for God's glory (Romans 8:28).

First Peter 1:3-9 says:

> Praise be to the God and Father of our Lord Jesus Christ! In his great mercy he has given us new birth into a living hope through the resurrection of Jesus Christ from the dead, and into an inheritance that can never perish, spoil or fade. This inheritance is kept in heaven for you, who through faith are shielded by God's power until the coming of the salvation that is ready to be revealed in the last time. In all this you greatly rejoice, though now for a little while you may have had to suffer grief in all kinds of trials. These have come so that the proven genuineness of your faith—of greater worth than gold, which perishes even though refined by fire— may result in praise, glory and honor when Jesus Christ is revealed. Though you have not seen him,

you love him; and even though you do not see him now, you believe in him and are filled with an inexpressible and glorious joy, for you are receiving the end result of your faith, the salvation of your souls.

When suffering persists, here is what the Lord may be intending to do for us:
1. Increase our trust in Him: He wants us to have our ultimate peace in Him. He wants to teach us to trust Him more regardless of the events or circumstances in our surroundings. Put your trust in Him alone. If the Father allowed it, it must be good for you.

2. Strengthen our dependence on Him: The Father wants us to depend on Him and not in our strength or wisdom. So, when He notices that we are too dependent on our own resources and abilities, He may take some things away, causing us to suffer some pain or loss. It is His way of reminding us that we need to depend on Him alone.

3. Manifest Christ's life in us: Through persistent suffering, the Father intends to sift, sand, and prune what does not belong in order to reflect who we are in Christ.

4. Purify our hearts: Blessed are the pure in heart for they shall see God. The Father may use difficulties in order to purify us.

In your circumstances, through your loss and through the hard times, remember to remain like humble clay in the hands of the master potter's hands, that He may mold you and transform your life into a beautiful vessel fit for His holy use.

As earthly beings, sometimes we work hard to earn the favour of our employers, parents, or even friends. We think that these people's applause and approval is crucial to our happiness. But as believers, we are to strive for God's approval. David wrote in Psalm 31:19 that "How abundant are the good things / that you have stored up for those who fear you." So, friends, do not violate your godly principles in order to please others. Understand that every good thing that comes our way is from the hand of God (see James 1:17). Don't rely on others' approval. Discover God's favour by feasting on His Word, learning His ways, and practicing His principles. You will be amazed at how His kindness is already flowing in every corner of your life.

Chapter Eight:

BE CONSISTENT

Keep serving and honoring God consistently even in your moments of darkness, sorrow, discontentment, pain, loss, suffering, or uncertainty.

I had this sharp pain on my right side, coming at me randomly one Wednesday night. It was excruciating, and I could not use my right hand. I thought I was tired, and due to being pregnant at this time, I thought it was a muscle spasm, so I took an early rest and went to bed. Waking up almost every two hours of the night was rough. Eventually, I remembered to pray at around 2:40 a.m.; I called upon the master healer to heal my body as I had too many family, ministry, and work responsibilities—I had no time to be sick. I fell asleep in the middle of prayer.

When I woke up at 5 a.m. to pray, as is my usual routine, the pain had really subsided. On a scale of 1-10, it had fallen to a 3. Then I prayed again for God to heal me completely, and I trusted Him to answer me. After my morning prayers, I felt like the pain had fallen to a 1. I went about my day fine, but the tinge of pain was still there.

Thursday night after work, the pain returned, now back to something like a 7 out of 10. I told my husband that maybe I needed to visit the doctor as the pain might have been indicative of some deeper problem. We decided to wait and see; if the pain did not go away by the weekend, we would visit the doctor. Feeling tired and weary, I fell sound asleep.

Friday morning, I woke up to pray, calling upon the master healer to restore my health and strengthen me. I did not like visiting the doctor's office or the emergency room at the hospital. As I finished my morning worship and started my day, I suddenly felt absolutely no more pain. The master healer, my great physician, had completed His perfect work. I felt fresh, strong, and energized as if a dark cloud had been lifted off me. What a mighty God I serve!

It is God's desire that we be totally healthy, whole, and fit to go about our service to Him and to humanity. He wants to grant us every godly longing in our hearts when we seek Him wholeheartedly and obey His commands. Yes, we all can consistently live an abundant life full of His favour. He wants to bless us in the overflow. He wants to sustain us and provide for our daily needs. All He requires us to do is to be in consistent hunger and thirst for Him. His Word says that blessed are those who hunger and thirst for righteousness, they will be filled (Matthew 5:6).

If you are experiencing challenges with your health or maybe you and your family are consistently sick, seek the Lord earnestly in prayer and in faith. Maybe He wants you to get desperate for Him, or maybe He wants to deepen your relationship with Him. He will reveal His will for your healing in prayer.

Although not all sickness is a result of sin, some of it is. Remember the sores all over the body of Job: it was Satan afflicting him; he had not sinned. Remember the blind Bartimaeus in Mark 10, the beggar whose sight Jesus restored: he had not sinned. It was for God's glory that he was blind. However, recall Miriam's leprosy: she was struck with it by the Lord as punishment after speaking against Moses, the humble servant of God, for marrying a Cushite wife.

See the passage below:

> Miriam and Aaron began to talk against Moses because of his Cushite wife, for he had married a Cushite. "Has the Lord spoken only through Moses?" they asked. "Hasn't he also spoken through us?" And the Lord heard this.
>
> (Now Moses was a very humble man, more humble than anyone else on the face of the earth.)

At once the LORD said to Moses, Aaron and Miriam, "Come out to the tent of meeting, all three of you." So, the three of them went out. Then the LORD came down in a pillar of cloud; he stood at the entrance to the tent and summoned Aaron and Miriam. When the two of them stepped forward, he said, "Listen to my words:

'When there is a prophet among you,

I, the LORD, reveal myself to them in visions,

I speak to them in dreams.

But this is not true of my servant Moses;

he is faithful in all my house.

With him I speak face to face,

clearly and not in riddles;

he sees the form of the LORD.

Why then were you not afraid

to speak against my servant Moses?'"

The anger of the LORD burned against them, and he left them.

When the cloud lifted from above the tent, Miriam's skin was leprous—it became as white as snow. Aaron turned toward her and saw that she had a defiling skin disease, and he said to Moses, "Please, my lord, I ask you not to hold against us the sin we have so foolishly committed. Do not let her be like a stillborn infant coming from its mother's womb with its flesh half eaten away."

So, Moses cried out to the LORD, *"Please, God, heal her!"*

The LORD replied to Moses, "If her father had spit in her face, would she not have been in disgrace for seven days? Confine her outside the camp for seven days; after that she can be brought back." So, Miriam was confined outside the camp for seven days, and the people did not move on till she was brought back. (Numbers 12:1-15)

Repent of all sin, both generational and present sin. Ask for the cleansing of the blood of Jesus from all unrighteousness. Ask the Lord to break all generational sin that may be hindering Him from blessing and healing you in totality. The Lord's anger burns against individuals who hate and disobey Him, and He counts their sin against their children, and their children's children up to the third and fourth generation (see Deuteronomy 5:8-10). But those who keep honoring Him consistently the Lord honours with favour and protection.

I like sharing with the world through my music; the written and spoken word; what the Lord has done for me;

and about His goodness, grace, and mercies. Every morning as I do my worship, I am inspired to share on social media what God is teaching me through the Holy Spirit. In my ministry, though, I have been tempted to quit a few times. Occasionally, I think that if I maintained a low profile and just feasted on God's goodness without having to be out there telling it, maybe it would be less work for me and more privacy.

So, one time, I decided to feed into my thoughts, and I stopped sharing the Word on social media as often as I had done it: daily. I missed one day. On the second day as I read my devotional, *Wisdom From Above* by Charles F. Stanley, the Holy Spirit got me so disturbed by what He was teaching me…in fact, I felt as if the message in my devotional was a direct rebuke to my decision to quit sharing the Word as I do daily. This is what it said: "Today will you stand up to this challenge to help others grow in their relationship with Jesus? Not only are you able—it is Christ's command to you. So, look for others to raise up, and pray for God's help in leading them to greater faith and obedience" (149). I prayed and, in tears, apologized to the Godhead for my earlier erroneous decision.

I accepted Christ's command to lead others into greater faith and obedience and to help them grow into a deeper relationship with Jesus. Even as I write this book today, it is my prayer that the words in it will help draw you to a deeper relationship with Christ and greater faith in Him. He is a God who never changes. He remains the same yesterday, today, and forever. We may change, our circumstances may change, but His love for us is unconditional and constant. He wants to be intimate with you, beloved. He wants to show you how to survive your losses, consistently attract divine favour upon your life for every season, find perfect peace amidst life's storms, and thrive in a purpose-filled life.

Whatever you put your hands to do, do it consistently; do not give up on the way or jump ship when you don't experience immediate positive results. First, determine that it is God's will for you, then proceed without getting weary. If a relationship is God's will for you, pursue it. If your ministry or business is God's will for you, keep doing it. You may not see results in one year or two, but the Lord is working behind the scenes to process you before bringing you the results that He desires. He is taking the time to refine you and ensure that you have the capacity for the blessing, the success, and the promotion that He is about to bring in your life.

One thing is sure: He will not start a work in you that He cannot complete. What if you know that a relationship, a job, a career, or ministry is the will of God for you, but you are not happy in the middle of pursuing it? Stay on course. Why? Because the Lord will Himself clearly speak to you in a way that you can understand without a doubt if it is time for you to leave. He is a God who understands every fibre of our being. He knows us better than we know ourselves; therefore, He knows how to communicate with us in a way that we will understand. Consider David: he was anointed king many years before he functioned as one. In fact, he encountered terrible times at the hand of Saul including being hunted to be killed. His family was dysfunctional, and he endured many heartbreaks. He still became the king that he was—the man after God's own heart, through whose ancestry the Messiah Himself was born.

Abraham waited thirteen years after Isaac was promised to him. Joseph waited many years from the time God gave him dreams about his greatness, enduring being sold as a slave, being accused falsely of rape, and being thrown in prison. In his prison, he was still serving the inmates when his call to greatness finally arrived.

Keep serving and honoring God consistently even in your moments of darkness, sorrow, discontentment, pain, loss, suffering, or uncertainty. The favour of God will show up in His perfect time. Persevere in suffering; it is the testing of your faith, which produces endurance. "Consider it pure joy, my brothers and sisters, whenever you face trials of many kinds, because you know that the testing of your faith produces perseverance. Let perseverance finish its work so that you may be mature and complete, not lacking anything" (James 1:2-4).

The Lord does not waste any suffering that He allows us to go through. Here is how we benefit from the suffering:

1. He uses it to draw us to Himself.

2. It is a tool for eliminating all hindrances to our holiness, helping us grow in faith and making us increasingly Christ-like.

3. Our trials become triumphs when we trust the Lord. Through hardships, we can share in the holiness of Christ (see Hebrews 12:10). He disciplines us to bring us to the point where Christ's holiness is expressed and not suppressed in our lives.

4. Through hardships, we can learn to give thanks in all situations (see 1 Thessalonians 5:18). We learn to be thankful in all situations, even in suffering, because we know that the result will be good.

5. Through hardships, we can develop steadfastness (see Romans 5:1-5). Tribulation leads to perseverance; perseverance develops character, which gives us hope.

6. When we choose not to give up during difficult circumstances, we allow God to build our character, which He can then use to keep us going in our lives for the long term.

7. We participate in the sufferings of Christ so that we can relate with His life and experiences and humbly recognize how much we need Him. When we choose to trust Him, the Lord uses those trials in amazing ways!

PART III WORKBOOK AND SELF-ASSESSMENT QUESTIONS

1. Often the question we ask when faced by storms in life is "why me?" Why not you?

2. What is the one thing that has helped you move from denying your pain into accepting it?

3. Do you believe that faith can play a great role in you finding inner peace amidst your pain? How?

4. How are you making peace with your difficult circumstances right now?

PART IV:

THRIVING IN A PURPOSE-FILLED LIFE

Chapter Nine:

HIDE AND SEEK

You do not have to despair, because God's wisdom is unlimited, and His perfect wisdom is available for you. Trust Him completely and with every fibre of your being, because He will never lead you astray.

I kept running away from God after my divorce had gone through. I thought that I had messed up my life, so I needed to fix it by myself. I knew what the Word of God said about my life at that moment, but I made no effort to obey it. I was neither hot nor cold; therefore the Lord was spitting me out of His mouth and allowing the consequences of a life that's not dependent on God to teach me the lessons I needed to learn.

I pursued a series of relationships, and I enjoyed going to the club on Saturday nights to dance my problems away. I even indulged in alcohol every once in a while, hoping that I would forget my pain: the pains of divorce stigma, single mother stigma, and thoughts that I was a terrible failure in life. I was so broken that every friend I associated with would hear my heart crying out for acceptance and would read desperation all over my face. During the week, I worked hard at up to three jobs to make as much money as I could to afford my new lifestyle. By then, I was living in Fort McMurray in the days of the boom in the oil patch. The city was so lucrative that I could make easy money through side hustles in addition to my regular job. I prepared taxes for people, cleaned residential/commercial buildings for pay, cooked food items for sale, and even organized parties where I charged entry fees.

None of these indulgences seemed to heal my heart. I was constantly unfulfilled, discontented, and searching for more. Whenever I had some downtime, I wanted to scream because I felt helpless and not good enough. A friend of mine would visit occasionally to talk to me. I constantly explained to her my burdens over and over. I would narrate the challenges of dealing with my ex-husband while exchanging our son; the suspicious eyes of women at church who I thought looked at me with disapproval whenever I shook hands with their husbands, as was the custom to greet each other after fellowship; the feeling of disappointment regarding the dreams I had for having a successful marriage/family and so forth. She tried to comfort and encourage me, but as soon as she left the door, I would remain wallowing in self pity.

One time, I searched on Google the meaning of my symptoms. Some results that came up included depression. I decided to visit the doctors to see what they would advise. I was diagnosed with a condition called Post Traumatic Adjustment Disorder (PTAD). This is a condition characterized by tearfulness, feelings of hopelessness, and loss of interest in work or activities. Adjustment disorder is sometimes informally called "situational depression." The type of stress that can trigger an adjustment disorder/stress response syndrome varies depending on the person, but can include:

- Ending of a relationship or marriage
- Losing or changing job
- Death of a loved one
- Developing a serious illness (yourself or a loved one)
- Being a victim of a crime
- Having an accident
- Undergoing a major life change (such as getting married, having a baby, or retiring from a job)
- Living through a disaster, such as a fire, flood, or hurricane

The treatment recommended included therapy sessions with a counsellor and some anti-anxiety medication. I really don't like medication, so I did not use the drugs, but I went to the sessions with the therapist. The healing process was slow according to my assessment. I could feel positive during the sessions, but when I went back home, my life seemed unbearable. This condition is known to happen within three months of the stress trigger and should not continue beyond six months. However, my disorder continued beyond the six months, and I was referred to a psychiatrist for further diagnosis. At this point, I had lost my appetite, lost sleep, and could not get out of bed even during the day. I totally isolated myself, lost my job, and I was struggling to take care of my son. I also had suicidal thoughts. It was diagnosed as acute clinical depression. The psychiatrist recommended going to my home country of Kenya to reconnect with my family and loved ones, as well as exercising and volunteering at places of community service. Going home was more refreshing, so I pursued that option.

Friends, when faced with symptoms such as the ones I have explained, it is important to seek professional help. But in my circumstances, I needed something more than professional help. No drink, relationship, or doctor could cure the void—that God-shaped void that was in my heart. Deep down, I knew that God would deliver me—I did not know from what. I knew He would bless me—I did not know how. I knew He would fulfil my desires and give me contentment, but I did not know who He would use to achieve that.

One time, I had asked a pastor to pray for me. His response was that he was going to pray for me, but in addition to prayers, he wanted me to stop fighting for myself. I did not understand what he meant by that. All I knew how to do was fight for myself.

Later, it made sense what this pastor said. I finally gave up on my strength and wisdom, because for six years, no positive results had come out of my thinking that I had brought this mess to myself and therefore I needed to clean it all up by myself. I surrendered and accepted defeat. I would not be able to heal my own heart from divorce, depression, and suicidal thoughts. Therapy had also failed. So, I gave up trying to fight for myself. It was only by reconnecting with the Lord, by finding Him, and trusting His heart that I was able to find the assurance, healing, and restoration I needed.

It was a hit-and-miss process to begin with because I would pursue Him through prayer and His Word, then I would be faced with temptation and fall back again. I tried a few times to seek the Lord, but I was not able to completely trust Him yet. After my divorce, I thought that quickly finding my next relationship would fix my loneliness and heal my broken heart. So, in trying to find the next best relationship, I hopped from one dysfunctional relationship with a member of the opposite sex to another. None of them matured into a meaningful long-term relationship. The reason being that I was broken and had not healed from my brokenness; therefore, I was only attracting broken people.

Finally, I was tired of doing the same thing over and over again and expecting different results. I knew I needed to change something, but I did not know what the change was. I felt helpless and begged God to help me come to Him in totality so that He alone could fix my broken life. I confessed that, in my own effort, I was not able to come to Him. So, I took my broken pieces and handed them over to Him. I allowed Him to work in me, transform me, and fight for me. The battle was no longer mine but His. Jacob wrestled with the angel of the Lord till the break of day. Jacob had refused to let go of his strong will. When the angel realised that Jacob was now ready to surrender his will, he changed his name from Jacob to Israel and blessed him, as we see in Genesis 32:24-29:

> So, Jacob was left alone, and a man wrestled with him till daybreak. When the man saw that he could not overpower him, he touched the socket of Jacob's hip so that his hip was wrenched as he wrestled with the man. Then the man said, "Let me go, for it is daybreak."
>
> But Jacob replied, "I will not let you go unless you bless me."

The man asked him, "What is your name?"

"Jacob," he answered.

Then the man said, "Your name will no longer be Jacob, but Israel, because you have struggled with God and with humans and have overcome."

Jacob said, "Please tell me your name."

But he replied, "Why do you ask my name?" Then he blessed him there.

In the story of Moses, the Lord appeared to him in the form of a burning bush (Exodus 3). He told him to remove his sandals because he was standing on holy ground. Moses was obedient. He did not resist removing his shoes so that the Lord would speak to him and direct him for the mission he had. What if Moses had resisted? Would he still have been used? Then when the Lord spoke and told him that his assignment was to set the children of Israel free, Moses complained that he was too inadequate for the task. But the Lord insisted that He would be with him. He asked him to use what was in his hand, the rod, to carry out this mission.

Sometimes we resist the call of God. We resist His plan for our lives and His process. We look at our inadequacies like Moses. Or rely on our own strength and wisdom like Jacob. When we face extenuating circumstances and the squeezing that will sometimes happen in our lives, we become crushed and lose focus.

We become disoriented and distracted from the path of God. I now know that doing so only wastes our time and delays the fulfillment of the Lord's perfect purpose for our lives. Maybe the restoration that took six years for me would have taken a shorter time if I had been more submissive to the will of God rather than relying on my own strength.

Friends, the pain and loss you are facing today should not push you to give up and give in to self-destruction. It should not cause you to run further away from the Lord. Only He can fill the God-shaped void in your heart. He is the lover of your soul and His love is unconditional. He loves you regardless of your circumstances.

What a wonderful thing to have a relationship with Him. He knows what you are feeling and thinking even right now. He knows who you are and how you function. He knows your likes, dislikes, hurts, dreams, fears, insecurities, losses, and pains. He knows what brings you real joy and satisfaction, peace and fulfillment. As your maker, He knows everything about your life—your past, present, and future and how to make the very best life possible for you. You do not have to despair, because God's wisdom is unlimited, and His perfect wisdom is available for you. Trust Him completely and with every fibre of your being, because He will never lead you astray. Romans 10:11 promises, "Whoever believes in him, will never be disappointed" (author's paraphrase).

As I came to complete acceptance of my losses and sorting my re-connection to God, I wanted to know my purpose in life. What would God have me do in the earth? What was His ultimate plan for my life? I fasted and prayed that He would reveal to me clearly what His will for me was regarding marriage, ministry, and career. Then the Holy Spirit said to me, "I did not create you to get married or to work; I created you for my glory" (see Isaiah 43:7). I believed this with all my heart.

"Then how do you want me to live in order to honor and glorify you?" I asked again in prayer. I was led to Romans 12:1-2 (KJV). "I beseech you therefore, brethren, by the mercies of God, that ye present your bodies a living sacrifice, holy, acceptable unto God, which is your reasonable service. And be not conformed to this world: but be ye transformed by the renewing of your mind, that ye may prove what is that good, and acceptable, and perfect, will of God."

So, in order for me to know the good, acceptable, and perfect will of God, I needed to be transformed by the renewing of my mind, then I also needed to present my body as a living sacrifice to the Lord, holy and acceptable for His use. These verses completely blew my mind. I was willing and ready to obey them. I wanted to conform my will to the perfect will of God. This meant alignment to His Word and His statutes. It meant living righteously and denouncing all wilful and habitual sin.

When you want to discover the purpose for which you were created, you must seek to reconnect to the one who created you in earnest expectation of hearing from Him and in all sincerity be ready and willing to obey what He says. Sometimes we go to Him asking Him to show us His will—yet we are not ready to obey what His will is. This is sabotage to a purpose-filled life.

If you have not found the purpose for which the Lord created you, I encourage you right now to take a pause at this section of the book. Find a quiet place and seek the Lord in prayer. Open up your heart to His leading and prompting. Repent of anything that would hold you back from hearing His voice and then surrender your life totally to His guidance. If you don't get your answer, persist in prayer with earnest expectation of hearing from God. He will for sure show you His will and your purpose.

My prayers were answered through dreams and spiritual promptings. He may answer yours through how He orders your circumstances, through a friend speaking to you, through a preacher, or even through His Word when you read the Bible. He is a faithful God and He speaks.
One thing I have discovered is that if singing, writing, speaking, preaching, or teaching blesses, uplifts, encourages, or brings people hope, healing, and transformation, then you are spiritually gifted in that area. But if what you do does not bless or encourage

others, then it might be just something you enjoy doing, a preference and not a spiritual gifting. So, go forth and do what the Lord has burdened you to do in your heart, but don't forget to also consider the input of others. Their verification is an indicator that you are spiritually gifted in your area of interest.

Chapter Ten:

BEYOND BLESSED

You are a sign that points others to the God who transformed you—so live out your life.

When I finally found my life of favour and bliss—my marriage restored, my heart healed, my life established and strengthened—it did not end there. The enemy of my soul still tried his arrows of temptation on me. He occasionally brought doubt in my mind as to whether this was really the will of God. I occasionally grumbled when things did not look as perfect as I expected. I could fret when things that I wanted did not fall in place on my timeline. For a moment, I could get distracted from the plan of God for my life. But I knew better. I realized quickly that I was going down the wrong path when even prayer became optional, not mandatory.

When I came back to my senses, I offered dangerous prayers. I asked God to protect me even from my own self; I asked Him to help me not to take matters in my own hands but to allow Him to author my life according to His perfect will. Then I began to see things from His perspective. I learnt that everything He allows in my life is to teach me and to transform me into the vessel of honour that He wants me to be.

In this era of skyrocketing divorce rates, crime rates, and evil days, we are to undergird our families and jealously protect them by covering them with prayer. You see, friend, Satan knows that family is the unit that makes up the church, and therefore he would do anything to destroy one family at a time, knowing that he will eventually destroy the church. He uses the three most common family destroyers—communication, finances, and in-laws—to try and wipe out the church.

Hold onto your family closely, beloved. Be steadfast in patience and prayer. When the enemy succeeds in destroying you from inside your family, he knows he has completely won. Don't allow him! Let the words of Proverbs 3:5-6 always be a lamp unto your feet and a light to your path:

> "Trust in the Lord with all your heart
> and lean not on your own understanding;
> in all your ways submit to him,
> and he will make your paths straight."

As we continue enjoying the favour of God upon our lives, we know that every experience and everything that happened to us is more than worth it. The Lord does not waste any experience but uses every one to bring us to the point of our lives we are at now. We can never attain perfection, but we can be obedient and readily available and willing to be used for the Lord's glory and to enrich the lives of those around us.

I am humbled that the Lord could use me as His masterpiece/mouthpiece to lift Jesus and share what He has done and continues to do in my life, hoping that someone could be drawn to Him. Matthew 5:14-16 says that we are the light of the world. Therefore, we must let our lights shine so that others may see our good works and glorify our heavenly father.

When the Lord has finished working on His project of you and me, He wants to show us off. He wants us to be His trophy so that He can pat our backs and say, "Well done, my good and faithful servant." He does not want our lights to be hidden under the table. He has called each one of us and equipped us with everything that we need to carry out His vison over our lives. He has a solution to everything we face. He sees the end from the beginning. He is strategic and does not make any mistakes.

Favoured is who we are in Him. He says that when we submit our broken pieces to Him, He will do a new thing.

2 Corinthians 5:17: "Therefore, if anyone is in Christ, the new creation has come: The old has gone, the new is here!"

Isaiah 43:19: "See, I am doing a new thing! Now it springs up; do you not perceive it? I am making a way in the wilderness and streams in the wasteland."

He also says that eyes have not seen, nor ear heard, neither has it entered the heart of man the things the Lord has prepared for those who love him (1 Corinthians 2:9). It is Christ's command that we spread the good news of His perfect love and how He is soon coming to harvest His chosen ones. He will take His chosen ones to a new heaven and a new earth where there will be no more pain or sorrow. Everything will be made brand new.

Beloved, you are a sign that points others to the God who transformed you—so live out your life.

In John 12:32, Jesus says, "And I, when I am lifted up from the earth, will draw all people to myself." God calls us to honour Him and submit to His commands so others will be drawn to Him through us.

So how do we do this effectively?

1. Be willing to invest time with those in need.
2. Listen to others carefully with an open, compassionate heart.

3. Love others unconditionally.
4. Help those around you understand that their most important relationship is the one they have with Jesus.
5. Inspire others to be all they can be, helping them recognize the Lord's plan for their lives.

When you do these things, people will see your faithfulness and be encouraged and motivated to follow the Lord in obedience. Sometimes it's not easy, especially to love others unconditionally, but the Holy Spirit who lives in us will empower us. We must ask daily for a fresh anointing. God answers this prayer.

Have you felt the Lord calling you to ministry, but you have put aside His voice? Maybe He has called you to write a book, preach, sing, inspire/encourage others, serve in the church, open a children's home/senior's home, or something else. You see, friend, the Lord is pleased with our diligent obedience. Do not fear failure, inadequacy, or criticism. Don't concentrate on the difficulty of your circumstances. Simply focus on worshipping and praising the one who called you to the task. His wisdom is infinite; His love, power, and provision are available to you and the victory is yours. He will empower you to conquer whatever challenge will come along. Wherever the will of God calls you to, His grace is sufficient. The safest place to be is in the centre of God's will, and nobody can put you there but yourself.

Here you find peace, contentment, and a reason to be all that you were created to be. Through your pain and loss, acknowledge His sovereignty. Believe in His supernatural working power. He has your best interest at heart no matter how lonely, dark, rough, or dreary your life may look at this moment. He is not done with you. He is absolutely in control of your circumstances.

I know what you are thinking right now: you probably are saying that I have no idea how bleak your situation has consistently been. But listen, beloved, nothing is hidden from the master healer, the Lord. He knows your every need. He knows you so much better than you know yourself. He even knows how you are reacting right now as you read this book. He sees the depths of your heart. Just give it all to him. I love the lyrics in Lynda Randle's precious song "Give Them All to Jesus." This is what she says:

"Are you tired of chasing pretty rainbows?

Are you tired of spinning round and round?

Wrap up all the shattered dreams of your life,

At the feet of Jesus lay them down."

I hope that through these few words, you have found encouragement and strength to persevere through your pain and loss. I hope that you have learnt how to attract divine favour upon your life in every season. I am still applying the principles that I have written in this book in my own life. I pray that when the end comes and Jesus returns, we will all hear the "well done, good and faithful servant" words from the mouth of the Lord.

In the meantime, do not worry about the applause of fellow men here on earth. Love the Lord with all your heart, with all your strength, and with all you've got. And serve Him first and best. Honor Him always and He will do this: honour you right back with favour, anointing, courage, and peace that surpasses all human understanding. Give all the credit to God for all the work He has done and is doing in your life.

Chapter Eleven:

THE TRANSFORMATION

The area of your deepest pain can become the area of your greatest impact.

It was my last day of work before I embarked on my maternity leave to spend time with my soon-to-be-born baby. This pregnancy with our third baby Jeremiah had been the hardest one. My body was retaining so much fluid, and I was growing so big. Unfortunately, with a lot of water retention came much swelling on my legs, face, and hands. I was swollen to the extent that I was beginning to have nerves being squeezed. My hands began to tingle and occasionally got numb.

So that morning as I woke up to get ready for work on my last day, I just couldn't pull myself together. My body was extremely fatigued, and my muscles ached. I tried to have a warm shower to see if I would feel better, but I did not. I actually began to have blurry vision and a dull headache. Tears began rolling down my cheeks uncontrollably; I knew something was wrong with me. I urged my husband to take me to the emergency room for a checkup.

So, we drove Joshua, our eldest child, to school, leaving our daughter, Jessica, behind with my aunt who was living with us at that time. We then proceeded to the emergency department of our local hospital. As we arrived, we were admitted at the reception desk and asked to go right to the third floor, which was the labour and delivery ward. I explained my symptoms to the nurse, who immediately put me on a monitor to check my baby's heart rate and movements, while she also checked my vital statistics. My temperature was fine, but my blood pressure checked very high. I was shocked at how my pressure had shot up from 110/70 (which was my average during my prenatal checkups) to 179/105.
Thankfully, my obstetrician was on duty at the hospital that day, and she was called to examine me. With all the swellings, fatigue, headache, and now high blood pressure, she diagnosed me with preeclampsia, a condition that would cause the placenta not to function properly and was characterised by the symptoms I had. Having seen a friend of mine go through the same condition with her pregnancy, I was scared. Thankfully, my baby was almost at full term, thirty-seven weeks. This condition usually means that the baby will need to be delivered earlier than the due date for mother and baby to be free from health risks. I was given some drug therapy to help lower my blood pressure and scheduled

for early baby delivery three days later. We booked a follow-up appointment the next day at six o'clock in the evening to check my blood pressure.

When we arrived at the hospital the following day, I was feeling much worse than the previous day. My headache had returned, and I was feeling run down, fatigued, and so unwell. As they checked my pressure again, it had skyrocketed to 196/106. The doctor was beside herself. We could not fathom why it had gone up so high so fast. That night, I was not allowed to go back home. We had to get the baby delivered as soon as possible; it was risky to continue with the pregnancy. This was now thirty-seven weeks, two days.

The routine for labour and delivery was arranged, and I was on the way to having my baby boy three weeks earlier than scheduled. I called on my close friends to pray that everything would go well. The nurses were busy monitoring and keeping the pressure to a desired level as well as ensuring the baby was okay throughout labour. Four hours later, baby Jeremiah Baraka arrived safely at 1:49 a.m.

Unfortunately, I continued to struggle with high blood pressure after delivery. We were released from the hospital a day later as they tried to stabilize my blood pressure. My drug dosage was increased, and I was allowed to go home. The days that followed continued to be painful as I still struggled with high blood pressure. The drug dosage kept being increased, and the pressure was mostly resistant. Seven days into it, I prayed. I sought the Lord to show me the meaning of this struggle. I was not only physically drained but also psychologically. It was a bad place to be in because I was not enjoying my little bundle of joy, the gift that I was supposed to be enjoying.

As I prayed and surrendered myself with expectation to hear from Him, God showed me that I needed to dig deeper to find the purpose of my pain as opposed to asking Him to take it away immediately. While research has not really identified why 5-8 percent of pregnant women develop preeclampsia, there are things that I did or did not do that may have contributed to my condition. I did not rest very well throughout the pregnancy. I was busy with work, family, and ministry. In addition, I was asked to get rid of salt intake to avoid retaining a lot of fluid in the body—I did not pay attention to this instruction.

I learned five lessons from my pain that I will share with you and then discuss further the transformation.

1. God's character is revealed in a more personal way through trials. God is just but also merciful.

2. We cannot avoid facing the consequences of our wrong choices. But when we do face the consequences, we can ask the Lord to show us His circumstantial will. This is the will of God in the middle of our own unique life's circumstances. Simply put, it is God's plan B for us.

3. God allows pain in order to use it for our good and His glory. He does not waste any experience. Everything He allows you to encounter He uses to teach you something important.

4. We can have pain in order to relate with others facing similar pain. You can comfort others with the comfort that you yourself have also received. You will be able to say to others, "I have been there." Do you find my experiences relatable?

5. Pain invites you to pray and connect back with God in order to deepen your relationship with Him.

If you are ill, do not always accept your illness as punishment for your sins. The Bible says that there's therefore now no condemnation to those who are in Christ Jesus (Romans 8:1). God has forgiven you. It is the devil's scheme for you to carry your guilt around. Don't let the devil intimidate you and cause you not to live for all that God has called you. You've got to believe that no weapon formed against you shall prosper (Isaiah 54:17). Your victory is already assured.

One more promise from the Word of God was highlighted in my spirit during my illness: "But my God shall supply ALL your need according to his riches in glory by Christ Jesus" (Philippians 4:19 KJV, emphasis mine). I believed this word with all my heart and claimed it, and then I received my complete healing three weeks later.

You see, because of your relationship with Jesus, He will meet your EVERY need. Not only what you require for physical health and well being, but also for your emotional, financial and spiritual needs. He will satisfy your soul with love, acceptance, companionship, and worth as no one else can. Today I thank the Lord for His perfect provision including the healing of my high blood pressure illness and the illnesses of those servants that will read this word.

Are you experiencing pain or loss? Remain faithful, keep your heart pure, and keep your eyes open. David had to be humiliated by Saul before he was honoured as king. In fact, I dare you to try transforming your pain into purpose. Find the meaning of your pain, find growth opportunities through your pain, and learn how you can transform that pain into purpose. Recognize that your pain can become your platform. The area of your deepest pain can become the area of your greatest impact.

As we have discussed throughout this book, pain is common to all of us, but dealing with it is not. Some of us may choose to numb our pain by engaging with addictive substances and/or behaviour while others embrace and deal with it from the core, uprooting not only the symptoms but also the cause of the pain, therefore developing inner strength and a purpose-filled life.

I would like to suggest to you five tools that can help you navigate successfully through your pain or loss. You can use these tools to transform your pain into purpose. The tools are not conclusive but a guideline or a starting point. As you pray and consider your unique circumstances, you may be convicted differently to author your own process and tools to navigate through your own pain, and that is very much okay. For easy remembering, I have come up with the acronym ACTED for the five tools.

1. **Alignment to the Word**
2. **Consistency**
3. **The Wait**
4. **Esther's Fast**
5. **Dangerous Prayers**

ABOUT THE AUTHOR

Up until now, Eunice has been working as an accountant. She is transitioning into a full-time role in ministry. She has started a movement to share Christ's message of hope, healing, and transformation through her music and the written and spoken word in order to help women and men to grow in relationship with Jesus and lead them to greater faith and obedience. Her movement aims to show you that there are blessings in brokenness and that you can navigate successfully through your pain while attracting divine favour, finding perfect peace amidst life's storms, and thriving in a purpose-filled life.

She is the founder of Divine Voice Foundation, a non-profit company that serves her community, and the author of *Broken but Blessed*. She has also recorded three gospel music albums. Eunice and her husband, Richard, are blessed with three amazing children: Joshua, Jessica, and Jeremiah. They live in Edmonton, Alberta, Canada.

To access *Broken but Blessed* or any of her music albums, you can head over to [www.eunicekemunto.com,](www.eunicekemunto.com) and you will be redirected to the right platforms.